St. Helena Library
1492 Library Lane
St. Helena, CA 94574
(707) 963-5244

YEARBOOK

1800-
MOYUL

YEARBOOK

SETH ROGEN

CROWN
NEW YORK

Copyright © 2021 by Seth Rogen

All rights reserved.

Published in the United States by Crown, an imprint of Random House, a division of Penguin Random House LLC, New York.

CROWN and the Crown colophon are registered trademarks of Penguin Random House LLC.

LIBRARY OF CONGRESS CATALOGING-IN-PUBLICATION DATA
Names: Rogen, Seth, author.
Title: Yearbook / Seth Rogen.
Description: New York: Crown, [2021]
Identifiers: LCCN 2021004346 (print) | LCCN 2021004347 (ebook) |
ISBN 9781984825407 (hardcover; acid-free paper) | ISBN 9781984825414 (ebook)
Subjects: LCSH: Rogen, Seth, 1982- | Motion picture actors and actresses—Canada—Biography. | Motion picture producers and directors—Canada—Biography. | Screenwriters—Canada—Biography. | LCGFT: Essays.
Classification: LCC PN2308.R64 A3 2021 (print) | LCC PN2308.R64 (ebook) |
DDC 791.4302/8092 [B]—dc23
LC record available at https://lccn.loc.gov/2021004346
LC ebook record available at https://lccn.loc.gov/2021004347

Photo Credits
Page 5: Courtesy of the author
Page 35: Courtesy of MGM Media Licensing, BLOODSPORT © 1988
METRO-GOLDWYN-MAYER STUDIOS INC. ALL RIGHTS RESERVED.
Page 134, left: "Steven Spielberg" by Gage Skidmore is licensed under CC BY-SA 2.0:
https://creativecommons.org/licenses/by-sa/2.0/?ref=ccsearch&atype=rich
Page 134, right: Courtesy of the author
Page 167: Jeff Kravitz/FilmMagic, Inc/Getty Images
Page 211: Courtesy of Universal Studios Licensing LLC,
copyright © 2004 Universal Studios
Page 212, top: Courtesy of the author
Page 212, bottom: Cole Burston/Bloomberg/Getty Images
Page 236: Bob Riha, Jr./Getty Images

Printed in the United States of America on acid-free paper

crownpublishing.com

2 4 6 8 9 7 5 3 1

First Edition

Title page illustrations by Todd James
Illustrations pages 70, 147, 207, 246–249 © 2021 by Son of Alan
Maps © 2021 by David Lindroth, Inc.
Book design by Debbie Glasserman

CONTENTS

YEARBOOK

BUBBY AND ZAIDY

I wanted to try stand-up comedy. I imagine if most twelve-year-olds told their parents something like that, they'd be met with a healthy dose of skepticism. Fuck, if a thirty-year-old told me they wanted to try stand-up comedy, I'd probably do my best to talk them out of it.

Which makes it even more incredible that not only did my parents *not* scoff at the notion of it, they looked in the local paper and found a stand-up comedy workshop to enroll me in.

I loved comedy growing up, I think, because my parents loved comedy. They would watch *SCTV*; Billy Crystal's stand-up; *Ghostbusters*; *Ferris Bueller's Day Off*; *Planes, Trains and Automobiles*; *Uncle Buck*; *Home Alone*; *Coming to America*; *Big*; *Who Framed Roger Rabbit*; *Back to the Future*; *The Breakfast Club*; *When Harry Met Sally*; *What About Bob?*; and they would just laugh their fucking asses off, and I would laugh my fucking ass off, and if people were doing this for a living, then I was gonna try to be one of those people.

The workshop was simple enough: You'd spend a day learning the basic concept of stand-up joke writing, write a few jokes, and then, that night, you'd go to the Lotus Club, a local lesbian bar with what in retrospect was a very vaginal flower painted on its awning, and perform your jokes for the lesbians. My mother dropped me off outside; I walked into the class and, not surprisingly, was the only kid—the first of about a thousand rooms that I would walk into over the next decade where that was the case. I've been the youngest person in the room a lot of my life. There's something nice about having aged into my job. But still, I miss those days, because when you're young, the bar for accomplishment is so low, no matter what you do, it's pretty impressive. If you're young enough, just walking is considered a huge deal. My friends are thrilled when their kids *don't* shit all over their floors. As an adult, I get little to no praise for doing the same.

The teacher, a working stand-up comic named Mark Pooley, who looked exactly like Garth from *Wayne's World*, took the stage.

MARK: Nobody wants to hear about what you like. There's nothing less funny than hearing about the stuff you have fun doing. Fun isn't funny. Comedy is pain. It's struggle. So, when thinking of what to write about, don't ask yourself, "What's funny to me?" Ask yourself, "What bothers me? What frustrates me? What do I wish I could change? What can I just not fucking stand?!"

One answer popped into my head. At that point in my life, there was really only one answer: my grandparents.

I didn't get along great with them back then. Their real names were Faye and Kelly, but I knew them as Bubby and

Zaidy. Their last name was Belogus, which is by all means a hilarious last name. I remember being thirteen, hanging out at a friend's house, and telling him that my mother's maiden name was Belogus. His nine-year-old brother cackled loudly from the other room. "Sounds like 'Blow Us'!"

It sure does, I thought. *It sure does.*

When I was younger, Bubby and Zaidy just didn't seem that into me. I got the impression they liked my older sister, Danya, more than me, mostly because their words and actions made it wildly clear that they did. They were just nicer to her, which didn't really bug me that much, because I didn't love spending time with them.

Me and my better sister, Danya.

They were simultaneously tough and eccentric. My grandmother was born while her family was in a caravan fleeing Poland as World War I was breaking out. She got to pick her own birthday when she was a little girl because her parents didn't know her real one, which is some real Depression-era shit. How rough was Poland for Jews at that time? So rough that when they arrived in Winnipeg, a city in Manitoba that has swarms of mosquitos throughout the summer and debilitating ice storms throughout the winter, they thought, *This place is fucking great! Let's stay here.* My grandfather was born in Winnipeg. One of three brothers (the others named Curly and Pinky), he played professional football in the CFL and lied about his age to go to war. When I was about six, we were on a family vacation in Palm Springs and I cracked my toenail when I stubbed it in the pool. My grandfather said he would fix it, and then ripped off the entire nail. We had to go to the hospital.

I didn't really start spending a lot of time alone with my grandparents until I was ten and my sister was thirteen and getting ready for her Bat Mitzvah. She had to attend services every Friday, and I did not want to do that, so my parents would drop me off at my grandparents' apartment to hang out for a few hours while they went to synagogue with my sister so she could pretend to pray.

Every Friday night would play out the same. I would plant myself on Zaidy's La-Z-Boy and turn on "TGIF," ABC's Friday-night programming, which consisted of *Family Matters, Step by Step,* and *Hangin' with Mr. Cooper,* which are all shows that are, by any definition, fucking dope as fuck.

My grandparents would make me a turkey sandwich on challah bread and pour me a glass of chocolate milk, and then sit with me as they tried their hardest to follow what the fuck was happening on these shows.

ZAIDY: **Who's that guy?**
ME: **He's the dad.**
BUBBY: **Who's the dweeby one?**

ME: That's Steve Urkel.

ZAIDY: And what's that? A robot (pronounced "roe-bit")?

ME: Yes, Steve Urkel built it.

BUBBY: What's the roe-bit doing now?!

ME: It's pretending to be Steve to trick the girl he likes into hooking up with him.

(This show has not aged well.)

ZAIDY: Steve Snorkel?

ME: URKEL!

ZAIDY: And what's the show called?

ME: *Family Matters.*

ZAIDY: *Family Bladders?*

My grandfather worked in the engine room of a battleship in the Royal Navy during World War II, and as a result, was more or less deaf. He loved being in the Navy. He talked about it like most guys talked about their fraternity years. They would hang out, smoke cigars, talk shit, all while floating in thousands of tons of metal around the war-torn Horn of Africa. He arrived at Normandy on D-Day Plus One, but his favorite story was about figuring out that if you broke your rationed rum bottle *after* drinking it, you could say you broke it *before* and get a double ration. Anyway, he was deaf.

ZAIDY: *Family Crappers?*

BUBBY: He's saying *Family Campers!*

ME: No! I'm saying *Family MATTERS!*

BUBBY: Stop yelling!

ZAIDY: Who's yelling?

ME: YOU'RE YELLING!

This would play out for about two hours straight, and as maddening as spending time with them was, I couldn't help but think they were entertaining.

Because they grew up in the Depression, they would steal

EVERYTHING. Every time we went to McDonald's, they would empty the napkin dispenser and put them in a giant box that my grandfather kept in his van. If we were out at dinner and you heard my Bubby say, "Oh, this is a nice plate," you *knew* the next time you ate at their place, you'd be eating off that plate, because she straight jacked that shit. Knives, forks, you name it, they swiped it.

Another thing I noticed was that my grandmother kind of had a wispy white Afro that, when the light hit it, became see-through, leaving you with a VERY good idea of what my grandmother would look like if she was completely bald. And . . . it was horrifying.

I wrote three jokes about Bubby and Zaidy that followed the basic structure we were taught: Say the premise or the thing you don't like; say why you don't like that thing by making a humorous observation; then do an "act out," an impression of the target of the joke, bringing it all together.

My grandparents were hard to impersonate, so I thought I'd just go with a generic "old Jewish person" voice. It was a safe but ultimately good call.

The night came, and my turn to take the stage was fast approaching. I honestly don't remember being that nervous, probably because I was twelve fucking years old and wasn't even mature enough to *be* nervous. I've definitely gotten more in my head as I've gotten older and marvel at how I used to just barrel into these situations without much fear or anxiety. Kids can do that. It's like those very young Chinese acrobats you see, flinging their little bodies in the air, being thrown around, completely unaware of the stakes. If those kids knew what a torn ACL was, they wouldn't be letting those motherfuckers toss their little asses around like that. And if I had known the pain and shame that goes along with putting yourself out there creatively and being rejected, I probably wouldn't have been so excited. But I didn't, so I was.

I took the stage. The lesbians' eyes locked on me.

"So . . . people ask me what the hardest part about being Jewish is. The persecution? The repeated attempts at systematic annihilation? Nope. The hardest part about being Jewish is . . . the grandparents."

They laughed. And thank fucking god they did, because if they didn't, I'd be one *very* frustrated videogame-store employee right now. I continued.

"My grandparents argue all the time, but they're both deaf, so they don't know what the other one is arguing about."

Time for the big, quasi-anti-Semitic act out:

"Hey, Kelly! Pass me a pillow!"

"What? I'm an armadillo? Why would you call me this animal?"

"What? I'm not wearing flannel!"

Small laugh but enough to keep going (which could also be the title of this book).

I went on: "My grandmother has a thin white Afro, and when the light hits her hair a certain way, you can see right through it and she looks bald. It's weird to see what your Bubby would look like completely bald. She looks like Gandhi in a pink floral tracksuit."

I finished it off with a joke about the stolen napkins that got a so-so laugh, and then I fucked off.

The lesbians loved me. A guy who worked at another comedy room gave me his card and asked if I would perform there the next week.

All those times I was dreading hanging out with my Bubby and Zaidy suddenly became something else. Something new. They were fodder. They were . . . material! I also began to suspect that maybe, just maybe, they knew they were being funny.

They would come and watch me perform from time to time, and not only did they not mind when I made fun of them, they got pissed off when I didn't.

Bubby: Where were our jokes? We're not funny anymore?!

Me: Don't worry. You're still plenty funny. I gotta make fun of Mom and Dad, too.

Zaidy: Ahh. Your mom and dad aren't as funny as us!

They were really my first significant comedic inspiration. My muse. Or, more accurately, my Jews (or Juse? Can books have alts? Seems like it!).

As they got older, I realized how much they did love me, and I appreciated more and more how genuinely hilarious they were. I started to see that among their friends, my Bubby specifically was considered a fucking riot. She swore, she drank, she laughed, she didn't take herself too seriously, but she also wasn't afraid of having hard conversations.

Bubby: All my friends are dying! The bastards! Don't they know I want to play mah-jongg?!

I remember when I was around twenty, we went to my cousin's Bat Mitzvah. At this point my Bubby must have been in her mid-eighties. My dad thought it would be funny to keep filling her glass of wine whenever she wasn't looking, so she thought she had maybe two glasses when she had actually downed about nine. She was SHITFACED. Like, drunk-college-girl shitfaced. We had to carry her out to the car, one arm around me, the other around my dad, as she drunkenly yelled, "I love you guys! You're the greatest!" She puked on the ride home.

My Bubby never really slowed down. She lived till her late nineties and was for the most part sharp and aware the whole time. Maybe too aware. Aging can be scary, and it seems like a lack of awareness can be a gift sometimes— a gift my Bubby never got.

"I'm old. I'm going to be gone soon. But it's okay. I'm ready. It's scary, but I think I'm ready."

"Don't worry," I would say, holding her hand. "I'm gonna stuff you and put you in the living room. It'll be like you never left."

She would laugh and cry a little at the same time, and so would I.

They're both gone now, but they shaped me in more ways than I can ever know and, thankfully, in one I definitely do: I wrote my first jokes about them.

When I was about to move to L.A. to be on *Freaks and Geeks,* I was getting a lot of advice. People love to give sixteen-year-olds advice, especially ones who seem to be at the precipice of a new life chapter. My teachers told me to keep up with the curriculum. The stand-ups I knew told me to keep working hard, to perform every night if possible. My parents wanted me to stay humble and keep my priorities straight. My friends wanted me to make good stuff that they would want to watch.

But it's my Bubby's advice I probably think of the most.

ME: I'm moving to L.A.

BUBBY: Oh yeah?

ME: Yeah. I'm gonna be on a TV show, and I'm probably just gonna try to stay there to see if I can make it in comedy.

BUBBY: Oh yeah?

ME: Yeah . . . so . . . any advice?

BUBBY: Sure.

She took my hand and smiled at me. "You give those sons of bitches hell."

BONANZA

My dad is from Newark, New Jersey. He somehow manages to be simultaneously bald and always in dire need of a haircut. My mom is from Vancouver, British Columbia. She's overfunctional, but also a Kundalini Yoga instructor who exudes peace and calm. As I've touched on, they're both the descendants of Jews who fled people trying to kill their asses in Eastern Europe, which can be said about most Jews in North America, but probably more eloquently.

My dad has OCD and Tourette's syndrome. He's constantly pacing around, swaying back and forth like a metronome. I also have a very slight case of Tourette's. It's something I actually recognize in a lot of other people who very likely aren't diagnosed and just feel "twitchy." I feel twitchy all the time. Like I have an itch that needs to be scratched. People with eyebrow furrows, clenching of facial muscles, clearing of the throat, flaring of the nostrils—I get exactly how that feels. For the most part I can control it, but I notice myself doing some twitchy shit from time to time.

My dad never had or wanted a traditional career, and his attitude toward work is refreshing in that he unabashedly hates it. None of his self-worth comes from what he accomplishes from a career standpoint. He thinks being a good person and helping others (something he's done throughout his life to a heroic degree) is a better way to get that, and I wish I'd inherited more of this to go along with the uncontrollable eyebrow furrows.

I have two half brothers by lesbian mothers. They were family friends who used my father as a sperm donor. The fact that those women looked at my dad and thought, *Great genetics there,* is confounding but ultimately complimentary. And I'm very glad they did, because my half brothers are great. Better than I am in most ways, making me feel a bit like some sort of "Schwarzenegger/DeVito" situation went down with the sperm, but I'm not sure the science behind *Twins* is totally sound, unlike the science behind *Junior,* which adds up completely.

My dad is super-specific about a lot of things but mostly about his socks and his food.

He essentially wears the same socks every day, white Champions. Over the years he noticed that when the socks became mismatched from their original pairs, due to the fact that they all looked the same, you'd wind up with a real variation of socks as far as wear and tear goes. Some socks were thin and aged, some brand-new and fluffy, but all were white Champions. It started to bother him that sometimes he'd be wearing socks with greatly varying feel from one foot to the other. So he developed a system. Whenever he bought a new pair of socks, he'd number them: 1–1, 2–2. The same number on each foot of the pair of socks. That way, although they all looked the same, he'd be able to maintain consistency when it came to the integrity of his socks from foot to foot.

It was a BIG topic of conversation in my house. It obviously made the process of sorting his laundry way more complicated, so he'd always have to do it himself, and it took him hours. My friends would come over and he'd be standing over the washing machine, pairing up the socks, every once in a while screaming to my mom, "Have you seen a seven or a nine?! I can't find them!"

It was *so* weird that when my mom's friend saw an ad in the paper that read, "Wanted for documentary: people with bizarre household-chore management," they instantly thought of my parents.

My dad got it, but my mom was a bit insulted. She was on the phone with her friend.

MOM: Why did you think I would be interesting?

FRIEND: Because of Mark's weird sock thing!

MOM: Oh, that makes perfect sens—

FRIEND: And, because of how messy your house is all the time!

Yes. My house was messy. I wouldn't say dirty but kind of . . . cluttered. There were always little piles of things everywhere. I'm not saying this is a Jewish tendency specifically, but almost every Jewish parent's house I've been to is like this. Nothing is put away. Everything is laid out in organized little stacks that are everywhere. Jews like to see all their belongings. We like to know what we've got at all times, just in case we gotta pack up shop and get the fuck out of town.

The crew came and filmed my parents talking about

housework and got shots of my dad organizing his socks and of all our little stacks and piles. It seemed like a cheap little Canadian documentary, so none of us really thought about it much—until my parents started to get recognized on the street by students.

STUDENT 1: Holy shit! You're the sock guy! (To Student 2:) It's the sock guy! From the documentary!

DAD: What do you mean?

STUDENT 2: We saw it in class!

MOM: What class?

STUDENT 1: Sociology class! They show the Chore Wars documentary every year! It really unravels gender roles when it comes to housework! And that shit with the socks! That's INSANE!

It might be a narrow baseline of fans, but among Canadian sociology students, my parents were major celebrities.

My parents are passionate about marching and protesting against injustices and are usually on the same page about the issues, but not always.

In Vancouver, there was a guy named Bill Vander Zalm (pronounced "Zam"), which is a supervillain-ass name if I ever heard one. When I was about seven or eight, he owned a big farm/fair-type place with a train and some rides and shit that you'd drive by on the way to the airport. All my friends loved to go. They'd have birthday parties there, but my parents banned me and my sister from ever stepping foot on his property. Bill Vander Zalm was wildly conservative. He had tried to restrict abortion laws and campaigned to break up local labor unions, which really could not be more on brand for a man with the last name Vander Zalm. My dad fucking hated him.

We heard Bill Vander Zalm was participating in one of

those big chanukiah-lighting ceremonies that they do in cities sometimes, and my dad was pissed. As someone who believed Jews should be standing up against injustice and supporting unions and progressive agendas, he was being driven nuts by the whole idea of it. I remember my parents talking about going to the event.

DAD: We have to go!

MOM: I'm not going to go if you yell at him!

DAD: Well, there's no point in going if I DON'T yell at him!

MOM: Just don't go, then!

DAD: We have to go!

MOM: We're not going if you make a big scene!

DAD: I won't make a big scene! I'll just make my protest clear in a peaceful way. That's it!

MOM: Fine. But if you go crazy, I'm going to pretend I have no idea who you are!

DAD: Fine!

MOM: Fine!

We hopped in our Chevy and drove a few minutes to a parking lot, where a huge chanukiah had been set up with a stage in front of it. There was a crowd of a couple hundred people standing around waiting for the ceremony to start. As men in suits took the stage and prepared to speak, my dad started getting riled up.

DAD: There he is. That hypocrite. I hate him. . . .

MOM: Alright, that's it. We're going over here now.

She grabbed me and my sister by the hands and started dragging us to the other side of the crowd.

Then Bill Vander Zalm took the mic.

BILL VANDER ZALM: Hello, and welcome to the Jewish ceremony celebrating—

DAD: You hypocrite!!!!!

Everyone in the crowd turned to see my dad screaming.

DAD: **How dare you use the Jewish community to bolster your agenda! You don't stand for anything progressive! You don't care about oppression! You're a fraud!!**

Security came and started to kind of wrestle my dad away from the stage and out of the parking lot. A few local news crews were there to cover the event, and they ran over to my dad as he was being carted out.

My mom turned to me and my sister: "Don't move. Just stand here. Act like you don't know him!" We did. We stared forward and watched the candle lighting as we heard my dad ranting in the background.

DAD: **(barely audible . . .) Hypocrite! (barely audible . . .) How dare he?! (barely audible . . .) on the Festival of Lights no less?!**

That night, we gathered around the TV to see if the event would be covered. I remember being very skeptical. But as soon as the local news started, the first headline plastered on the screen read: "Local man goes wild at holiday ceremony!" Lead story. They showed footage of Vander Zalm taking the stage, and then my dad screaming from the crowd.

ANCHOR: **What started as a celebration of our Jewish community ended as an attack on a local businessman. Moments after the ceremony began, Vancouver resident Mark Rogen had some words to share.**

They cut to an interview with my dad, where he went off on Vander Zalm. I looked over at him watching. He couldn't have been happier. I looked back to the TV.

ANCHOR: **While many in attendance were obviously disturbed by the disruption . . .**

It cut to shots of terrified members of the crowd watching my dad rant like a madman. It then cut to a shot of me, my sister, and my mother, completely ignoring my father. The only ones in the entire crowd not looking in his direction.

ANCHOR: . . . this family somehow managed to be totally unfazed by the outburst.

A lot of my childhood revolved around food. Because of the Tourette's, I basically had ADHD, which is common. What wasn't common was my parents' approach to treating it. Instead of putting me on medication, they brought me to a behavioral dietician, who had this crazy thought that what you eat affects how you feel and behave. Basically, I didn't eat ANY dairy, wheat, or sugar of any type from ages five to eleven or so. The only fruit I could eat were pears, the lamest of fruit, because they have less sugar than all other fruit, because they're so lame. Even their shape is outwardly mocked, and there's for sure foods with funnier shapes (squash is the goofiest-looking shit ever!), which just shows how much people hate these fuckers. They're straight up getting picked on. I ate the most boring food on earth. The other kids loved to make fun of me, always being like, "Don't eat a banana around Seth or he'll go fucking crazy!" Which really stung 'cause it was kind of true. I mean, you could eat a banana *around* me, but if I had so much as a bite of one, I would go completely insane.

My dad essentially grew up in his family's kosher butcher shop in New Jersey and is now a vegetarian, so it would take maybe five minutes of therapy to uncover why he is so specific about food. We always had separate plates for meat and vegetarian fare, but he had no problem preparing meat or being around it.

My mom, who became a social worker and taught parenting skills, has a different quirk, where she has a phobia of starving to death. She treats every outing like she's climbing

Everest—planning around calorie intake, how many snacks per hour, tons of little baggies in backpacks with granola bars, jerky, crackers, gorp (a funny word for trail mix). My mother must go through around 2.7 million Ziploc bags in any given calendar year.

We would go out to eat a lot because nobody in my family had similar tastes, so it was impossible to cook "family dinners." We didn't have a lot of money, but we lived in a big city, so we could find affordable restaurants with something for everyone. Or I should say affordable restaurant, in the singular, because we pretty much only went to one at a time. We'd go there about four days a week until something made us move on to another restaurant.

The first place I remember frequenting was called Bonanza, and the reason we stopped frequenting it is cemented in my head forever. We fucking loved Bonanza. It was a buffet-style place that was a 5 percent nicer version of Sizzler, which still makes it about 85 percent *less* nice than all other restaurants. They knew us there. They knew all my dad's super-strange quirks: diet soda, no ice; lemon on the side; extra napkins so he can wipe up the table himself throughout the meal. You know, OCD shit. It felt like a little haven for us. Like Cheers, if it gave you terrible diarrhea every time you got home. Actually, maybe Cheers gave people diarrhea, who knows. They sure didn't emphasize it in the show, but it could have been going on in the background.

Vancouver didn't have a ton of terrible snowstorms, but in 1990 the city was walloped. We carpooled to and from school with a few other kids from Richmond, which is a smaller city just outside Vancouver. My dad had dropped us off in the morning, and throughout the day, snow dumped down. By the time he came to get me, my sister, and the Josephsons, there were a few feet of snow on the ground.

We piled into my dad's car, and as soon as we saw his face, we were spooked. He looked like he had just driven through some sort of *Mad Max*–style wasteland to pick us up. He was shook.

DAD: Alright! Buckle tight! It's crazy out there, and these idiot drivers don't know how to drive in the snow in this stupid city because you don't have any actual seasons here! But we'll make it! Hold on!

If you haven't driven in a snowstorm, it's terrifying. You can't see shit, and the car doesn't do what you want it to do. We inched along Oak Street toward the bridge leading to Richmond from Vancouver in total silence, which is how my dad always drives. No radio, nothing. "Who can operate a vehicle with music blasting?! Who can focus with all that noise?!" is something my dad likes to yell while he's driving.

DAD: Okay! Most of the idiots have gotten off the road, which is good! We're doing good! We're—

Suddenly, in the middle of the bridge, the car hit an ice patch and spun in a full 360, slamming into the snow that had built up around the divider.

DAD: Holy moly! Drat! Alright! Everyone okay?!

We were.

DAD: Alright! Let's try to get off the bridge!!

He inched down the back half of the bridge, and as soon as we crossed into Richmond, the roads were impassable. It started snowing harder and harder. He pulled over, sat for a second, staring off into space, then looked back at us.

DAD: Alright, we can't drive anymore. That's it. We gotta abandon the car. We're miles from any of our houses; it would

take us hours to get there. But . . . I think . . . about half a mile down that road . . . it'll be hard . . . but . . . I think we can make it to *Bonanza!*

Everyone's eyes lit up! Salvation! With an all-you-can-eat buffet and soft-serve bar (which is also what they should have called the bathroom. Hiyooo!).

DAD: Alright, zip up your coats! We can do this! Let's move!!

We followed my dad out of the car. The snow came up to our knees. Every step was an undertaking for our tiny bodies.

DAD: Come on! We can do it! This way!

My sister was wavering.

DANYA: Dad! No! We're not gonna make it! There's too much snow!

DAD: We'll make it! Bonanza's just around the corner! Don't give up! We're so close! You can order off the menu when we get there! Not just the buffet like usual! The *actual* menu!

DANYA: Whoa—the <u>actual</u> menu? Alright—let's do this!

We marched on, breathing hard, our feet cold and our socks soaked.

DAD: We're almost there! Come on!

We gathered our energy and rushed to the corner, my dad raising his arms in celebration as we climbed over a wall of snow into the parking lot.

DAD: Yeah!! It's right here!! We made it!! We—

He stopped in his tracks. His arms lowered to his sides.

DAD: No . . .

We turned and looked. There was Bonanza, shades drawn, lights out, a giant OUT OF BUSINESS sign plastered across its front doors. My dad dropped to his knees and bellowed to the heavens: "NOOOOOO!!!! BONANZAAAAAAAAA!!!!"

It was gone forever.

But thank god a Red Robin had opened nearby. And thank god even more that Red Robin had the brilliant idea to have unlimited French fries on their menu. From the ashes of disaster grew the roses of a new life.

❄ ❄ ❄

My mom and I were always close, which for a Jewish boy is probably the least surprising thing I could possibly write, other than saying that dairy messes with my tummy. She's the only child of my insane grandparents and somehow turned out to be considerate, progressive, levelheaded, emotionally honest, and wildly weird at the same time. We became a lot closer in 1997 when we went to Israel together to visit Danya, who was living on a kibbutz for a year. We arrived and got in our rental car. Driving in Israel was totally crazy, and we had to make it all the way across the country, stopping in a hotel thing for a night along the way.

My mom loves music, and we blasted Sublime and A Tribe Called Quest the entire way. (Again, it was 1997. Just be happy we weren't doing Da Dip.) We arrived at the hotel and it was not what we were expecting. Basically, it was a house. Thinking we were going to a hotel but arriving at a house in the middle of nowhere was shocking, especially in a pre-Airbnb era. We approached the front door and knocked.

A friendly Israeli man in his fifties answered the door: "Shalom! Baruch Falafel Latke!"

(This is not what he said, but they are Hebrew words I know, so they'll do.)

MOM: Uh . . . we don't speak Hebrew.

ISRAELI MAN: Shalom!

He gestured for us to follow him and led us through his house to a back room with two twin beds.

MOM: So, we stay here? In your house?

ISRAELI MAN: Knish! Yes!

MOM: Uh . . . okay. Perfect. Thanks.

The guy eyed us for a second.

ISRAELI MAN: No! Not perfect! I make perfect! Rosh Hashana!

He then started awkwardly trying to push the two heavy metal bed frames closer together.

ISRAELI MAN: I fix! I make nice!

We protested.

ME: No! It's not necessary!

MOM: Please! No! They're fine where they are!

ISRAELI MAN: Is fine. Is fine! I make one big bed! For nice couple!

It was then it occurred to both me and my mother that this man thought we were in a sexual relationship with one another.

ME: Is NOT fine!!

MOM: No! Not fine!

ISRAELI MAN: Exactly, like this, is not fine.

The Israeli made a sexually suggestive face to me.

ISRAELI MAN: I fix! Make it fine! Gal Gadot.

ME: No! Do NOT fix! We are not . . . uh . . . needing the fixing of anything!

ISRAELI MAN: Is fine! Matzoh! I do not judge! Is fine!

He wouldn't take no for an answer. He kept pushing the two heavy beds closer and closer until they made one big bed in the middle of the room. Unfortunately, it would be easier just to move the beds back ourselves than it would be to convince this man we weren't just a shy couple.

We laughed about it for the entire rest of the trip, and still do. Nothing brings you and your mother closer together than having an Israeli innkeeper assume you're fucking one another.

SONS OF COMMANDMENT

Jews have a lot of odd traditions.

They wear kippahs, which are funny little hats about the size of the palm of your hand that, I'm sure NOT so coincidentally, fit perfectly over a bald spot. Am I saying a major tenet of Judaism was formed to protect the vanity of balding Jewish men? Yeah. Yeah, I am.

They get circumcised, which I guess I've grown to have mixed feelings about. Do I have animosity toward my private parts? Not really. Do I sometimes wonder what it could have been like to have a penis that lived on in its natural state? Sure. I also think of my phantom foreskin, out there somewhere, penisless, and then I think, *It's probably better off.*

I think a lot of Jews wonder what it would be like to experience a foreskinned penis. Is it better? Is it worse? Is it, in general, warmer? It would, by definition, be *more* penis, which is probably something every guy would be on board with. I've thought about starting a business where I sell prosthetic foreskins to Jews so they can feel what it would have been like to have non-Jew junk. It would be called Gentile Genitals and it would make a fortune.

When Jewish people turn thirteen, they have Bar or Bat Mitzvahs, depending if you are a boy Jew or a girl Jew, respectively. You get up onstage at temple in front of everyone you know and read from the Torah in a crazy singsongy tune that I'm 100 percent sure has no musical logic to it in any way, shape, or form, which is objectively humiliating. To make things worse, you have to prepare for a fucking year for this shit.

There are three good things about having a Bar or Bat Mitzvah:

1. A party. You get to have one after your service, and at that age, I'd been led to believe that having a party thrown in your honor is a fun thing, which is something I've since greatly reconsidered.

2. You get gifts. Often in the form of money. Which is a thing that I wanted to have to buy things I didn't have. A good haul could get you several THOUSAND dollars. That's right. All 'bout the Binyamins, baby. (I'm sorry.)

3. In order to have a Bar Mitzvah, you have to go to Bar Mitzvah class, which sucks. BUT you also have to be invited to all the Bar and Bat Mitzvahs of everyone in the class, and there were about sixty kids, so that's essentially an entire year of going to parties every single weekend, which was a pretty exciting prospect.

I was entering high school the following year, and I had one goal: I wanted to have a girlfriend/be a boyfriend, which I had never had/been before. I'm not sure I really wanted a girlfriend for the right reasons. It wasn't sexual, as the idea of even taking my shirt off in front of a girl horrified me. I remember hearing about Orthodox people having sex through a hole in the sheet and thought, *Man, that would solve a lot of my problems.*

I wanted a girlfriend because I was scared shitless about going to high school, and I thought it would make me seem like less of a loser and therefore less likely to be eaten alive by older kids. It's like Edward Norton wanting all his friends to beat him up before he went to jail in the Spike Lee movie *25th Hour.* Norton's character, Montgomery "Monty" Brogan, is about to serve a seven-year sentence for selling drugs. He figures he might as well go in there on the right foot, which in his case meant looking like a guy who had a proclivity for having the living shit kicked out of him, which I guess is a good thing in prison? Anyway, he had a scary situation ahead of him, and he did what he felt he had to do to prepare.

Similarly, I thought, *What better way to enter high school than in a relationship, firmly staking my claim as an adult? I'll have social status, a teammate, and everyone will like and respect me, and my life will be great.*

Not the right reasons.

At this age, the only way I knew to get a girlfriend was through dancing. Not just any dancing. Slowwww dancing. It was the only way to really gauge how a girl felt about you, since actually talking about your feelings was unheard of. You would slow dance, and the closeness of your bodies indicated how likely you were to become a couple. If there was full-body contact, you were dating. If there was grinding, you were essentially engaged.

But in order to dance to a slow song, you first had to navigate a minefield of *not* slow songs. And you did NOT want to dance to a fast song with a girl. With guys it was fine, and funny dancing was preferred.

Luckily, it all became pretty predictable, because every single Bar or Bat Mitzvah had the same DJ play the party, with basically the same playlist. Nirvana was popular, and all the boys would mosh wildly to "Smells Like Teen Spirit," until Austin Bell got a concussion at Steven Glanzberg's Bar Mitzvah and they stopped playing it.

"Cotton Eye Joe" is by a Swedish band called Rednex, whose gimmick was that they dressed up like the villains in *Deliverance,* which is an odd choice for a pop group. But say what you will, "Cotton Eye Joe" is a great song, in a "this song is not great but fun to listen to for two years straight" kinda way.

I don't know if "gimmick pop" is a genre of music, but if it were, I'd be a fan. "She Blinded Me with Science," "Blue," "Scatman," "Barbie Girl"—if there's an odd conceptual buy-in required to enjoy a pop song, I am your audience. Unfortunately, these types of bands don't always have longevity, and Rednex themselves were haunted by the success of their only major hit. So much so that almost every other song on their album *Sex & Violins*—which I purchased—sounded exactly like "Cotton Eye Joe." There was a song called "Old Pop in an Oak" that is so derivative, I'm tempted to say that Rednex should be ashamed of themselves, but the truth is . . . I understand the pressure to give people more of what they want. That's how you wind up with movies like *Neighbors 2.* "This one worked! Everyone loved it! They want more! Not

NEW more! Just MORE more!" I've been there, Rednex. *Neighbors 2* is the "Old Pop in an Oak" to *Neighbors*'s "Cotton Eye Joe," and I honestly think I've experienced personal growth now that I've gotten that off my chest.

But no song would create the controversy that was created by "Mony Mony," originally by Tommy James and the Shondells and later covered by Billy Idol. I'm sure you know the song: "Here she comes now, singing Mo-nay Mo-nay," followed by three strong drumbeats: "BAH! BAH, BAH!" This pattern essentially continues for the rest of the song.

Now, I couldn't tell you why or how, but for some bizarre reason it became a tradition to fill in these "BAH! BAH, BAH!"s with the words "Hey, motherfucker, get laid, get fucked!" over and over.

BILLY (SINGING): Here she comes now, singing Mony Mony!

ROOM FULL OF TWELVE-YEAR-OLD KIDS: HEY, MOTHER-FUCKER, GET LAID, GET FUCKED!

BILLY: Shoot 'em down, turn around, come on, Mony!

ROOM FULL OF TWELVE-YEAR-OLD KIDS: HEY, MOTHER-FUCKER, GET LAID, GET FUCKED!!

And so forth for the entire five minutes and two seconds of the song, which is an obscene length for a song that repetitive.

So, there's a lot of weird shit surrounding this phenomenon. One is, like I said, for the life of me, I could not tell you where this came from or why. There was no Internet, none of us had been to a Billy Idol concert—we didn't even know who he was. It was just this bizarre thing, as though the collective consciousness was like, "This song needs these words, and we're gonna put them in there." I found an interview where Billy (first-name basis) said that he heard that it started in British frat houses in the late eighties, so how it made it to the Vancouver Jewish scene in the early nineties is beyond me.

Obviously, the parents didn't like it, so they started to tell the DJ, "Before you play the song, warn the kids not to say the bad words, and tell them that if they say the words, you won't play it."

He would. "Now, before I play 'Mo-nay Mo-nay,' I just wanna say that you should NOT say the thing you wanna say during the song, or I will NOT play the song anymore."

I remember thinking, *Who gives a fuck? This song came out before we were born. The only reason we like it is because it gives us a chance to scream the word "FUCK" at the top of our lungs, which is great. So, if we can't do that, we don't need to hear this shitty song; just play the Rednex some more. That shit is great.*

But the real goal was a slow song. "End of the Road" and "I'll Make Love to You," both by Boyz II Men, were great options. "Can't Help Falling in Love" by UB40 wasn't bad, but their bullshit quasi-Jamaican beats made them almost tread into fast-music territory, so they were risky. Also, the fact that the world accepted a white British band that just did synthy reggae covers of other songs is truly fucking amazing in retrospect.

Hands down, the ultimate slow song to feel out if you really had chemistry with another person was "I Swear" by All-4-One.

"And I swear . . . by the moon and the stars in the sky . . . I'll be there. (I'll be there!!)" It's ironic that so many young Jewish men and women had their first feelings of intimacy sparked by what I've since learned is a decidedly Christian song.

My Jewish elementary school had uniforms, so I'd never really had to decide what I wanted to wear. Bar and Bat Mitzvahs were my first chance. And I was jumping right to formal wear.

We didn't have a lot of money, so pretty much everything would come from thrift stores, which Vancouver had many of, the best being a gigantic place called Value Village. I was a strange dresser and found fashion inspiration in odd places. I was obsessed with rap and hip-hop, so the only piece of clothing I had at this point, apart from my school uniform, was a black leather L.A. Raiders cap that I convinced my parents to buy me after I saw Ice Cube wear one in a magazine. But that wouldn't fly for a Bar Mitzvah, so I had to find inspiration elsewhere.

The movie *Tombstone* came out in 1993, and while it wasn't a massive box office or critical hit (*The New York Times* called it "morally ambiguous"), it made an impression on many, mostly due to an amazing performance by Val Kilmer that was publicly praised by President Bill Clinton, which is the single most nineties sentence one could write. As 1994 rolled around, a young me was smitten with not only Kilmer's performance as Doc Holliday but the entire Western aesthetic. The result? A fuckload of vests.

I could not own enough vests. I'd have bought more torsos just to wear them all if it were an option. I loved me a vest. It packed me in, gave me shape, and, most important, kinda made me feel like a cowboy who was dying of tuberculosis, which Val Kilmer had somehow made seem superawesome. I also wore a pocket watch, which in a truly impressive act of delusion, I convinced myself was cool as fuck.

It wasn't.

Time after time, weekend after weekend, a slow song would come on, boys would ask girls to dance, girls would ask boys to dance, and I'd generally find myself standing on the side watching it all happen, spinning my pocket watch like some sort of 1920s Mafia snitch. And again, it wasn't just the clothes. I was, in general, awkward, ill-motivated, and just not at the right level of maturity for any type of romantic relationship.

I remember being at Julia Morinis's Bat Mitzvah and noticing two other guys also standing on the side, watching with longing as the other kids had fun. *I'm one of those guys,* I thought. *What a fucking bummer.*

And then I noticed two OTHER guys. They weren't standing on the side, watching with longing. They actually seemed like they wanted nothing to do with the girls or the boys or the dancing or any of that. I knew them from my Bar Mitzvah class. Their names were Sammy Fogell and Evan Goldberg, and I knew we'd be going to the same high school.

Sammy was one of those thirteen-year-olds who look like they're about nine or ten. People called him "Psycho Sam" because he had a crazy temper. Evan was gigantic for his age and had sort of a Baby Huey meets Homer Simpson–ish quality to him. He had this habit of yanking on the collars of his shirts, so they were always all stretched out and saggy.

I watched as they scavenged for discarded glow sticks, cutting them open and pouring the glowing noxious goop that was inside all over their hands.

I went over.

ME: What are you guys doing?

EVAN: Pouring this glowing shit all over our hands and shit so they glow.

ME: Awesome. Did you think of splattering it all over your clothes? Then they'd glow, too.

Fogell and Evan looked at each other, then back at me.

FOGELL: **Fantastic idea.**

Actually, I thought, *I'm one of* these *guys.*

We spent the rest of the night, and many others, collecting glow sticks, cutting them open, and slathering ourselves with the (highly toxic) contents. We refocused our energy from dancing to slow songs to drinking discarded beers and martinis and smoking cigarette butts. A few times, I think, I even saw some other kids looking at *us* with longing. But then "I Swear" would come on and they'd go dry hump while we slowly poisoned ourselves with glowing radioactive sludge. Up till then, all the friends I had were out of convenience. I hadn't really selected any of them. I was just near them all the time, so they were my friends. But me, Fogell, and Evan chose each other.

The Bar Mitzvah year ended, and high school was next. I didn't feel ready. I was still scared of taking my shirt off, scared of everything in general really.

But at least I wasn't alone.

THE KARATE YID

I started taking karate because I was afraid of getting beat up, which is ironic because pretty much all that happens in karate is you get beat up.

I was obsessed with martial arts. Jean-Claude Van Damme, the Muscles from Brussels, was my favorite, followed very closely by Steven Seagal, who, I think, even though he passes himself off as an Italian with the last name "Seh-gall," is actually a Jew with the last name "Segal," which is great re-branding.

I loved the film *Bloodsport,* which (insanely) is allegedly based on the true story of Frank Dux. It's about an American soldier—he's from Brussels in the movie, which is never explained—who enters the most elite underground fighting competition, the Kumite. The ultimate villain in the film was an actor named Bolo Yeung, who was a bad guy in countless martial-arts movies, going back to Bruce Lee, and was easily identified for having the biggest fucking pecs I've ever seen in my life. The dude was half pec. Over my bed, the last thing I saw before I fell asleep and the first thing I saw when I woke up, was a poster from the film that featured Van Damme, mid–jump kick, nailing Bolo in his chest, the implication being that his kick was SO strong, even those massive pecs were useless to stop it.

I also loved *The Karate Kid,* which I related to more, because, well, it's about a white kid who learns karate. In that film, Daniel LaRusso is being bullied by a group of kids in his high school who all do karate. But not just any karate: Cobra Kai karate, a dishonorable school of fighting that teaches truly unsavory techniques, like the foot sweep. Daniel meets Mr. Miyagi, a bonsai salesman with a fucking dope-ass car collection, who ultimately teaches him the honorable way to fight, and he kicks the shit out of the Cobra Kai bully using an awesome crane kick.

I was a soft kid, and I was generally scared. And by soft I

don't mean just, like, mentally soft. I was literally soft. I had a Pillsbury Doughboy quality to me. I seemed flaky and delicious, like you wanted to poke me and make me giggle.

When I was about seven years old, I was with my mom at the Vancouver Jewish Community Center, where she was taking an Israeli dancing class. When the class was over, I noticed a karate class starting in the same space, and I knew a kid in it! He seemed so psyched. I remember looking at the kids in their *karate gi* and being like, "I fucking want that shit."

My mom enrolled me, and I met the teacher, who thank god was NOT Jewish. I'm not saying a Jewish dude wouldn't be a great karate teacher . . . actually, yes, I'm 100 percent definitely saying that a Jewish dude wouldn't be a great karate teacher.

My teacher was Shawn Ho, a Japanese Canadian guy who was, simply put, the most badass motherfucker I've ever met in my life, and I owe a lot of my confidence to him. He was short. Smaller than me. He was friendly, light, and funny. His age was literally impossible to tell, but I think he was in his fifties at the time, which is crazy. He seemed like he could take anyone out with the flick of a finger.

We did Kyokushinkaikan karate. Our motto was "Never give up. Always do your best." A solid starting place in general.

I learned a good lesson in karate, which was that just by not quitting, I'd progress. When I started, I was the worst of about twenty kids. After two or three years, I hung in there, and eventually everyone else who was ahead of me when I started dropped out of the class, and I became the highest-ranking student.

Slowly, though, I started to realize that our school of karate maybe wasn't modeled on the ones I grew up watching in movies. Or, at least not the school of karate that you were rooting for.

SHAWN: Never be afraid to foot sweep! If you have to, grab hair, gouge eyes, spit in their face, grab their balls and twist! Whatever you have to do to win.

Holy shit . . . I was in the Cobra Kai.

My theory was really cemented when I was about twelve and we went to a tournament for the first time.

ME: Why haven't we gone to more tournaments?

SHAWN: Oh, we're banned.

ME: Oh, cool. Why?

SHAWN: Some stupid bullshit.

ME: Cool. Anything I should know about this? Any special rules or anything?

SHAWN: Nope. Just win.

My first event was a sparring competition where I was facing off against a much bigger, older, and meaner-looking dude. I could tell just from how he bowed that his technique was much better than mine. He had crisp and explosive movement. The ref yelled for us to start, and the guy extended his arms and advanced on me, at which point I did a little trick I had where I smacked my opponent's arms out of the way with one hand and punched him in the throat as hard as I could with my other, which worked exactly as well as you'd think.

The guy dropped to the ground, gasping like he was drowning. I raised my arms in victory—only to find the ref and judges looking at me with genuine rage.

JUDGE: TURN YOUR BACK AND KNEEL!!!

I was being publicly shamed as they checked on the other kid, who caught his breath after a few seconds.

I got disqualified from the competition and went back to Shawn, expecting to be yelled at.

ME: I lost!

Shawn motioned to the other kid, being tended to by his sensei. He smiled. "Doesn't look like it to me."

❖ ❖ ❖

I was about to start high school, and, again I'll say, I was scared shitless. I had gone to a Jewish elementary school, which was pretty sheltered and not at all diverse, in that it was all Jewish kids. I would be going to public high school at Point Grey Secondary, which was across town and was going to be VERY different. About three thousand kids attended, and it was incredibly diverse, about 60 percent of the kids being from Asian countries.

In Vancouver, there's no middle school, so grades eight through twelve are all together, and that feels fucking insane if you're on the "eight" end of that spectrum. It was like going to school with full-grown adults. There were kids with beards. Like full fucking beards. There was a pregnant girl, which was sooooooo far outside what I was expecting. It's like if a Minotaur went to school with us. I was shocked.

There were fights, stabbings, beatings, which seems odd for a high school in a lovely part of Vancouver's west side called Kerrisdale, but it happened. A few weeks into school, a kid was making a pipe bomb in shop class and blew his hand off. All to say, compared to Jewish elementary school, it felt like a lawless free-for-all.

To add to the rough transition, like I said before, we'd always worn uniforms in grade school—blue pants and white shirts, making us all look like little abstract versions of the Israeli flag. I'm not sure making young Jews so easily identifiable is ever a great idea, but that's what we wore. And because of the Jewish uniforms, or "Jew-niforms," I never really had to think about how I dressed "casually," and the few times I had were kind of disastrous.

When I was around eight, I was obsessed with Weird Al Yankovic and made my mom get me the leather jacket that he's wearing on the cover of *Even Worse,* which is by default also the jacket Michael Jackson is wearing on *Bad.* But for the purposes of this story, let's say I idolized Weird Al and not Michael Jackson. (Who would have thought the guy named "Weird Al" would ultimately become the less controversial figure.) I remember walking into school, black leather jacket over my blue-and-white uniform, chrome zippers and buttons shining under the fluorescent lights, everyone looking at me like I was the biggest fucking idiot in the world.

I skateboarded, so I thought, *In high school, I'll dress like a skater.* Also, I was really into Nirvana, Green Day, Soundgarden, Marilyn Manson, Korn, and White Zombie, and I'd go downtown to buy band T-shirts every chance I could. I dyed my Jew-fro bright green, which kind of faded and turned a pukey yellow color, so I basically made my big entrance into Point Grey looking like a giant fucking clown.

High school meant freedom. We could essentially leave campus whenever we wanted. There was no real security at all and various kids had free periods throughout the day, so the result was a constant flow of students in and out of the school, which made it easy to skip class and explore Kerrisdale. It was like our Middle-earth, a mystical and dangerous world.

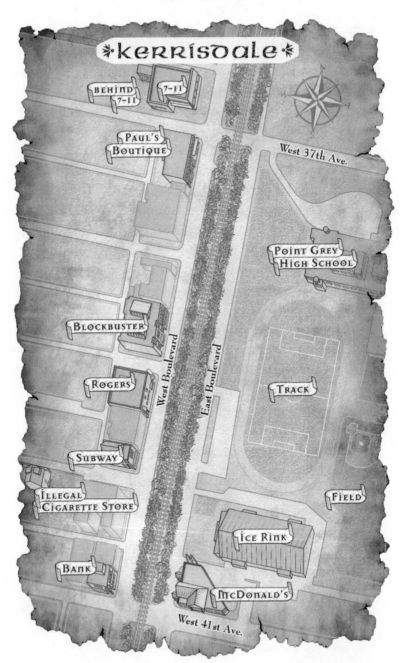

✳kerrisdale✳

BEHIND
7-11

7-11

PAUL'S
BOUTIQUE

West 37th Ave.

POINT GREY
HIGH SCHOOL

BLOCKBUSTER

West Boulevard

East Boulevard

TRACK

ROGERS

SUBWAY

ILLEGAL
CIGARETTE STORE

FIELD

ICE RINK

BANK

McDONALD'S

West 41st Ave.

The 7-Eleven was the main hub of social life. To get there, you had to cross the railroad tracks, which had only a few entrance points because of the thick blackberry bushes that ran alongside them. On that side of the boulevard, there was Paul's Boutique, the skate shop, and two video stores, a Blockbuster and Rogers, which was a Canadian chain. Then there was Subway, where a girl was rumored to have blown six guys in the bathroom. Right up from Subway on a side street was a Chinese convenience store where they'd sell cigarettes to kids of any age. You'd cross back over the train tracks to get to McDonald's. Then, heading back to the school, you'd pass an ice rink, which connected to the back of the school.

My main priority was not getting killed, followed by making friends and having fun.

I asked my karate teacher what the best way to deal with high school fights was.

SHAWN: Don't get in any! There's almost never a fight you can't avoid if you're smart. But if you do find yourself in a confrontation, just knee 'em in the balls, then smash your forehead into their nose as hard as you can.

The two places violence would mostly break out were behind 7-Eleven and at house parties, which you'd think would mean I'd just avoid those things, but I did not. In fact, they were probably the two destinations I was aiming for the most—behind 7-Eleven because I could smoke weed there, and house parties because I could get drunk there.

After school, everyone would go to the 7-Eleven and hang out on the loading dock behind it. It's where *everything* happened—fights, drug deals, kisses, thefts, treaties. It was an intimidating and exhilarating place to be. I didn't even have the nerve to go there for the first few weeks of high school. And the first time I did go, someone stole my hat. It was like the scary bar in Western movies—no matter how terrifying it was, people still always hung out there. I used to watch Westerns and be like, "Why are people at this bar?! You know there's gonna be a shoot-out. Go hang out somewhere else!"

But, like the bars in those movies, there was no other option, so you HAD to hang out there. Those cowboys just wanted to see their other cowboy friends and maybe get one of those drinks that made the bar sizzle when the cup overflowed. Sure, they knew there was a chance they'd get shot and fall off a balcony onto a table, but it was worth it. That's how it was behind 7-Eleven. You wanted to smoke a bowl before lunch and prayed you didn't get hit by some errant fist as you did.

We would also shoplift, a lot, which might be an inherited trait. Once I faked a seizure on the floor, distracting the staff, allowing around seventy kids to fill their pockets with everything they could grab before the manager realized I was fucking with him. That got me banned for a week, which, in retrospect, was a pretty light punishment.

I don't drink now, but from when I was around thirteen to twenty-three, I'd drink as often as I could without derailing my life in a meaningful way. And even though parties were dangerous, they were the best place to actually ingest your alcohol with shelter from the elements.

It wasn't *that* hard to get alcohol, but we had to get creative.

We'd get a "Boot," which is when you ask someone outside the liquor store to buy it for you, or we'd ask an older sibling or cousin or something, which worked fairly reliably.

You could raid your parents' liquor cabinet and make a

"shit-mix" of little bits of booze from each bottle, which works when you're younger, but once you're drinking significant amounts, it doesn't really do the trick. Or, you could steal a whole bottle, but that's dancing with the devil in the pale moonlight, which IS a quote from Tim Burton's *Batman*.

There was a liquor delivery service, "Dial-a-Bottle," but you needed a house without parents to receive the goods, which wasn't always available, and you didn't want to order to the party itself, because they'd take hours sometimes.

At some point, we noticed that a lot of bars stored kegs of beer on the loading dock in the back, so one day we hatched a plan to steal one. We grabbed it, rolling it away under the cover of night. Then we realized we didn't have a pump, so we used a hammer and screwdriver to knock the little pressure ball out of the top. We couldn't keep the keg in any of our homes, because it was just too big to hide, so we poured the beer into as many containers as we could find— Tupperware, old yogurt containers, detergent bottles, two-liter soda bottles, empty jars, shit like that—and we kept the beer, unrefrigerated, in our bedrooms as we drank it over the next few weeks.

We loved to play Edward Fortyhands, wherein everyone at the party had to duct-tape forty-ounce bottles of beer to each hand and not remove them until they were empty. We'd do the Century, where everyone took one shot of beer a minute for one hundred minutes in a row, which equals about eight beers in an hour and forty minutes. Either way, there were too many fucked-up kids in one place, and shit got real crazy quite regularly.

At one party, some kids stole the entire washer and dryer from a house. They had a dolly and everything, so it seemed weirdly premeditated. I have no idea why they did it or what they ended up doing with them, but I sure as hell wasn't gonna stop them. They couldn't have needed the appliances for themselves—they were high school kids. Even if their parents needed a new washer and dryer, it's hard to imagine they'd be psyched if a set showed up late one night after their son returned from a house party.

Cocaine wasn't a very big part of our scene, but at one party over winter break, we got a bunch. I had never done it before, and I didn't love it, thank god. Things got super out of control, as they tend to when a bunch of people are coked up, and the cops came.

I was standing on the front porch, watching in horror as one of the officers walked up to the door.

COP 1: **What's going on in there? Mind if we look around before we send you home?**

I glanced back over my shoulder to see the kids inside starting to clean up the cokey mess, but it didn't seem like it would happen in time.

The cop was walking into the party when suddenly his partner called out from the street.

COP 2: **Hey! You're not gonna believe this—we're fucking stuck!**

The other cop stopped, and we all looked toward the street, where their cruiser was, in fact, stuck in the snow in front of the house. The cop in the car was jamming the gas, spinning the wheels, not moving an inch.

COP 1: **Fuck.**

COP 2: **Do we call it in?**

COP 1: **No! Absolutely not! We'll never fucking hear the end of this!**

The cop looked at me and some other kids standing by the front door, then back at the car.

Cop 1: I'll tell you what, kids. You help us push our cruiser out of the snow, we won't break up your party. We'll just leave.

I looked at the kids around me.

Me: Fucking DEAL!!!!

Our young bodies fueled by cocaine, we pushed the cruiser out of the snow and watched as it drove off, which is a very Canadian way for that story to have ended. Also, I'll add that cocaine is a fucked-up drug and I don't recommend that people get into it. On top of being terrible for you, it makes you not fun to hang out with for *anyone* who is not also on cocaine. I've been to so many bachelor parties where the shroom people are constantly coming up with ways to herd all the cocaine people into one little area so they can just bother each other with their dark rants instead of the rest of us.

But as far as giant shitshows involving young people getting super-duper fucked up, there was no bigger party than Arts County Fair. It was a fundraiser put on by undergrads at the University of British Columbia and was THE biggest student-run event in Canada. It was essentially a giant beer garden in an outdoor field hockey stadium. Although you were supposed to be nineteen or older to attend, it was VERY quickly discovered that the hand stamps they used at the entrance were really easily transferable from one hand to another if you wet them a little bit. And since the only people manning the door were the undergrads themselves, it was basically a complete free-for-all. Pretty much every kid from every high school would skip class and go to Arts County

Fair, press their hand against someone's to transfer a stamp, and get shitfaced all day. And we couldn't be more psyched for our first year, 1997.

Me, Evan, and Fogell went early in the morning, skipping our first class and taking the bus to UBC. We licked our hands and pressed them against the hands of the first of-age kids we saw, and that was it, the floodgates were open. We were in a giant beer garden. And we fucking went for it. Beer after beer after beer after beer. If you could physically make it up to the counter and show your stamped hand, they would give you beer.

About an hour into the day, I ran into a counselor I had from summer camp, who gave me a weed cookie, which I devoured. Around noon, we were all incredibly fucked up and I lost Fogell and Evan in the crowd. I tripped and stumbled around looking for them for a couple hours, and at around 2 P.M. most of the other kids from our school started to arrive. A huge line formed at the entrance to the beer garden, and that's where I saw Evan, sitting in a chair right outside the front gate. He had been removed from the premises. He was holding his head in his hand, puking all over the place, as dozens of kids from our school waited in line, watching and laughing their asses off. It was playing out in slow motion. Pointing, hysterics, BLARRCH, Evan puking again.

This is how he will be remembered throughout the rest of high school, I thought. *A puking loser. Already done by the time everyone else showed up. What a bummer for him and, by proxy, me.*

Then two paramedics appeared, holding a stretcher, and walked toward Evan. This was going from bad to worse. How humiliating. He was literally gonna be carried out in front of everyone.

But then, right when it seemed like his high school reputation was being publicly burned at the stake, Evan Goldberg flipped the fucking script and did the stuff of legend.

He was loaded onto the stretcher in a daze, and as he was being carried away, he snapped out of it, looked around, and screamed, "NOOO!! I. NEED. MORE. BEEEEEEERRRRR!!!!!!!!!"

He jumped off the stretcher, shoved aside a paramedic, and RAN. Everyone in the huge line cheered as he bolted past them! He grabbed a beer mug from someone's hand and leapt over the barrier leading into the beer garden. Then he disappeared into the crowd, chugging his beer as he went. If they made commemorative stamps for amazing achievements in getting fucked up, Evan's Arts County Fair rally would be one of them.

☙ ☙ ☙

During the first few years of high school, some of the other kids heard I did karate, which had the complete opposite effect than I hoped it would. It kinda made everyone *want* to fight me. It just seemed unlikely that I was able to defend myself, so the instinct was to test my abilities.

It's like when you see a puffer fish at the aquarium. You're like, "That goofy fucking thing can really make itself dangerous? Bullshit! I gotta see this for myself!" Your instinct is to agitate it to see if it'll actually do its thing. That was me. I was a puffer fish. Goofy-looking in the first place, and when trying to defend myself, somehow even goofier-looking.

My quest to not get my ass kicked out in the wild was probably never put to the test more than in the case of "Smokey" McPherson.

Smokey was not his real name. His real name was Eric,

but Eric had an obsession with the movie *Friday*. It came out in 1995, and if you were a thirteen-year-old pothead named Seth, you and everyone you knew were pretty fucking into that shit.

Friday is about a recently fired dude named Craig (Ice Cube, let's not get into him for now), who lives in Compton with his parents. His best friend, Smokey, in a truly amazing performance from Chris Tucker, is a pot dealer who works for a dangerous upper-level dealer, Big Worm. Smokey wants to cheer up Craig, so they smoke all of Smokey's weed, which he's supposed to sell. Big Worm finds out and the two have till the end of the day to pay him back. It's fantastic, and *Pineapple Express* wouldn't exist without it.

Eric McPherson was so into it, he dressed like Smokey every day, in khakis, a black T-shirt, a gold chain, and a black baseball hat, which was objectively nuts to begin with, but this motherfucker then went so far as to ask people to call him "Smokey." Giving yourself a nickname is almost always incredibly whack, and nobody called Eric "Smokey" unless they were making fun of him, which was sad because it all stemmed from the fact that he just desperately wanted to be cool. Out of respect, I'll call him Smokey for the rest of the story . . .

At a party the previous week, Smokey had hooked up with a girl in our grade, Yael, who had an older brother in twelfth grade, Harris, who was intent on kicking the living fuck out of Smokey. Smokey was on high alert, and whenever you were with him, you knew you were hanging out with a marked man, so I for one tried to avoid him at all costs.

One day, me and Fogell had eaten lunch at McDonald's and were about to head back to school. Smokey was at McDonald's, too, and saw us heading back.

SMOKEY: **Hey, I'll walk with you guys!**

Me and Fogell knew he was just looking for cover, but it was hard to come up with a reason to say no.

ME: Uh . . . sure.

We were walking along the railroad tracks when we looked up and saw the worst possible sight: Harris and about five of his friends coming toward us.

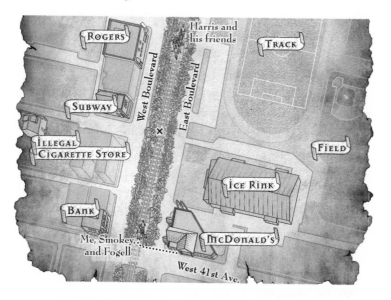

The blackberry bushes were trapping us, so there was no-where to go but back the way we came, which would mean turning around and running for about a block and a half, which seemed like a bad idea. I'm not sure why it seemed like a bad idea, it just did. Maybe turning our backs on them seemed scarier than knowing where they were? It's like with wild animals. They teach you that turning and running is bad, which I guess I believe to an extent, but eventually there HAS to be a point when it's better to run. Like in *The Reve-nant*, there was a moment when Leo would have for sure been better off if he'd run. How could he not have been?

Smokey was rightfully terrified, and so were me and Fogell.

SMOKEY: Oh shit. That's Harris. He's Yael's brother. He wants to fucking kill me, man.

ME: Oh shit is right. They're fucking coming.

FOGELL: Fuck! I knew we shouldn't have walked back with you!

SMOKEY: Why not?

ME: Because of this exact shit!

SMOKEY: Should we run?

FOGELL: No! That'll make it worse. Maybe this is a test. Like, to see if you actually are worth beating up or not?

SMOKEY: My instinct is that I am!

ME: You never know. Maybe running proves your guilt?

We kept walking toward one another. We were maybe forty-five seconds away from contact.

SMOKEY: If they want to fight me, will you help me?

ME: No.

FOGELL: Absolutely not.

SMOKEY: Why the fuck not?!

ME: Fuck you, that's why! Harris is insane!

SMOKEY: But we're friends!

ME: Sort of!

FOGELL: Neither of us have, like, ever been to your house before.

ME: Yeah! I've never even met your parents!

SMOKEY: You wanna come over tonight?

FOGELL: No! Too late! We're not that good friends! Not good enough to get fucking killed!

SMOKEY: PLEASE!

ME: . . . Okay. We'll try.

FOGELL: Yeah . . . okay.

Our two groups collided, and they absorbed him like a swarm. Me and Fogell didn't even break stride. We just kept walking, afraid to look back.

ME: **We really pussied out of that one.**

FOGELL: **Sure did.**

ME: **Smart choice.**

FOGELL: **I don't regret it one bit.**

I finally glanced back to see Smokey being flipped onto the hood of a parked car, his feet sticking vertically in the air before slamming down with a crash. We saw him later that day—black eye, ripped shirt—telling a bunch of kids in the hall how Harris and five of his friends had kicked the shit out of him on the railroad tracks.

I was happy for him. For that moment, he was actually the coolest guy in school.

PORNOGRAPHIC ENTERTAINMENT

This chapter is about pornography, but at no point will I get into masturbatory details, so you don't have to worry about that shit. Anyhoo . . .

I think a lot about those little sea turtles that you see on TV—the ones that are born on the beach, instilled with a natural and unwavering instinct to find the ocean, and eventually they do, but they struggle. That's kinda how it was with me and pornography. I wanted to see it. I wanted to enjoy it. Yet I could not find it.

There was no Internet, and when we finally got Internet, it was really slow and only on the family computer, which was in our living room, so it was hard to access, pornographically speaking. But we had "Superchannel," which was the Canadian version of HBO, and it played a lot of movies. I noticed that some of those movies had nudity. So, like many twelve-year-olds at that time, I got a blank VHS tape and slowly, over the course of a few months, made sort of a sex scene/nudity mixtape. It had a scene from the Steven Seagal movie *Under Siege,* where a woman jumps out of a cake topless; a clip from a sex scene in the Jean-Claude Van Damme film *Double Impact;* the naked woman beating up Gary Busey in *Point Break;* and an intense sex scene with Lorenzo Lamas from a film called *C.I.A. II: Target Alexa,* which he also directed, so good on him, I guess.

Around that time, I was skateboarding with my friends one day, and we noticed that the convenience store nearby had a *Playboy* in the magazine rack. There was only one option, which was to steal that shit. A plan for a heist was hatched. I would purchase a bottle of Jolt Cola, shake it up too much, and open it in the store, making it spray everywhere, creating a diversion. My friend would hide the magazine behind his skateboard and leave while I was wiping up. It worked like a goddamn *Oceans* movie, and by that I mean so flawlessly there's no dramatic tension in any way, shape, or form.

We ran to a park to look at our loot: a *Playboy* that featured a fifty-four-year-old Nancy Sinatra, which was . . . surprising? It wasn't bad, per se. It just wasn't really what we were expecting. She was a solid fifteen years older than our parents at the time, so I guess it wasn't hitting the notes we'd hoped it would. Also, it was a *Playboy,* and therefore rather tame.

When I was thirteen, it all came together, which is the grossest way I could have said that. I did a play that was being put on by the Chinese Cultural Centre in Vancouver's Chinatown, which in 1995 was a pretty rough neighborhood. I was standing outside, waiting for my mom to pick me up on a rainy day, when I looked down into the gutter . . . and there it was. A porno magazine that for some insane reason had been discarded in a pile of wet pages. I looked up the block and saw my mom's SUV turn onto the street. I reached down and grabbed a handful of sopping pages and shoved them in my coat pocket as my mom pulled up. I hopped in, feeling like I'd just found a briefcase full of gold. *I hope whoever's that was doesn't come back looking for it!* I remember thinking.

When we got home, I ran up to my room and carefully tried to salvage the remains of the magazine. It was like the scene in the movie *Titanic* where Bill Paxton handles Jack's drawing of Rose after fishing it out of the ocean. I used tongs and tweezers to pull the ball of wet pages apart, and I laid it all out on my bed to dry.

Over the next few hours, the pages cured into sort of a porn jerky. They were brittle like potato chips—you really had to be careful. Not only were they precious, they were delicate, which only added to their overall mystique. To this day, my brain intrinsically links fragile ancient documents with sex. The *Indiana Jones* franchise is very stimulating to me. Don't even mention the Dead Sea Scrolls.

What's odd is I actually have known a lot of people over the years who have found porn on the street, in parks, things like that. I knew a kid in high school who found a garbage bag full of porn on a baseball diamond near his house. Who is doing this? Who is taking huge amounts of porn and dumping it in playgrounds for kids to find? Is this some unspoken paying-it-forward cycle that has happened for years? Do porn companies do it to get kids hooked? Is Larry Flynt just tossing wet *Hustler* magazines out his window into gutters as he drives around Canada? 'Cause if he is, that would be some smart shit, because it got a lot of people I know invested. It personally sent me on a long road.

Before Internet porn became a thing, I basically engaged in "trading circles" with friends, where we would all share whatever porn we had so everyone got more variety. A side effect was that you got a slightly too intimate look at your friends' sexual proclivities and preferences. Also, sometimes you just got some weird-ass shit.

Once in early 2002, my friend gave me a DVD titled *Cum Dumpsters 2*. I had not seen the first *Cum Dumpsters* but felt like I could probably pick up the story. I was a little nervous to watch it, but I figured what the hell.

I'll never forget what happened next. . . .

I put the DVD in my Compaq laptop and waited for the movie to load. The screen went black, and then the image of an American flag, waving in the wind, slowly faded in. Then, in elegant cursive, appeared the words:

Dedicated to those who lost their lives on September 11th.

And then the opening credits for *Cum Dumpsters 2* started, which was a startling tonal shift to say the least. I like to imagine they really just wanted to do *something* in the wake of 9/11 and that was their only outlet. They were like, "We can't let people watch *Cum Dumpsters 2* without knowing that we, the filmmakers, understand the climate that we're in and that we're sensitive to it! Otherwise, the whole *Cum Dumpster* franchise will just seem tasteless!"

The "see your friends' taste in porn" effect has been multiplied by a billion with things like Pornhub, because you can easily see what global proclivities are—and they are fucking weird. A LOT of people seem to want to fuck their stepsister. It's insane. It seems to account for the storylines of, like, 90 percent of produced porn. Maybe it's because I never had stepsiblings, but I just don't get it. If you ever run into me on the street, and you have insight into why someone might want to fuck their stepsibling, please, for the love of god, do not talk to me about it. That would be a horrible conversation to have with a stranger.

Another thing about porn is that it seems like one of the last bastions of outward racism when it comes to the titles and categorizing of its movies. The use of the word "oriental" is still rampant. It's like my grandfather named the clips. I get that fetishes are fetishes, so you gotta get specific, but have some sensitivity.

The comments on porn sites are incredible. They're actually nicer than the comments on most corners of the Internet. I guess people who are jacking off are generally in a good mood, but the comments are so supportive and complimentary.

"What a great dick!"

"Her butthole is so pretty!"

"His load is dope and ropey!"

It's so nice!

I have no judgment of sex workers whatsoever. I honestly couldn't be more grateful for them, and over the years I've found myself working with them regularly. We don't have a ton of nudity in our films generally, but there is some, and early on we realized that a lot of "mainstream" actors are not incredibly psyched about getting naked on camera; it's more just something they're willing to do for a particular role.

We found that if we have a role that requires some sort of nudity, we should hire porn actors. The dynamic is completely flipped. They're generally super-thrilled to be on the set of a mainstream movie, getting to do something funny, and whatever we're asking them to do is definitely gonna be one of the least intrusive things they've been asked to do that week. It's a win-win-win. Over the years, I've had the pleasure of working with Stormy Daniels, Jenna Haze, Nautica Thorn, Bambino, and a lot more.

One of the peaks of my porn-related endeavors happened in 2003 when I went to the AVN Awards in Las Vegas, which is like the Oscars of porn, mostly in that it's fucking long as fuck.

There were ninety-four categories, each announced live, and they got VERY specific. Some were:

Best Three-Way Sex Scene

Best All-Girl Sex Scene

Best Oral Sex Scene

Best Couples Sex Scene

Best Solo Sex Scene

Best Anal Sex Scene

Best Foot Fetish Sex Scene

Best Ethnic-Themed Video

Best Non-Sex Performance

Best Specialty Big Bust Video

Best VHS Packaging

Best Vignette Series

Best Tease Performance

Most Outrageous Sex Scene (Something called *Love in an Abbatoir* won this, which sounds fucking gross and appears to be misspelled in the actual movie.)

The show itself lasted about five and a half hours, and in a lot of ways it was like any other award show but with a slight porn-y twist. You know how at, like, the Golden Globes and shit, Halle Berry will make some deep comment, and they'll cut to Tom Hanks nodding thoughtfully, which appears on a big screen to the side of the stage? At the porn awards, they did a similar thing, but whenever they cut to someone in the audience, that person would see themselves on the screen and pull out their breast and start licking their own nipple or something like that. It really split focus.

Another takeaway was how genuinely moved the winners were. I've been to the Academy Awards a handful of times, and I can say with absolute certainty that these porn performers were more emotional while accepting their awards. They would cry hysterically as they gave their speeches.

"I can't tell you all how deeply moved and touched I am to be given the award for Best Anal Orgy. . . . This just . . . this just means so much to me!"

And it should! They really deserve these awards. The winner of Best Anal Orgy worked harder for that statue than Meryl Streep ever has. Sure, she learned to talk like Julia Child, but can she stick nine dicks in her ass while keeping good light for the cameraman? This is not a rhetorical question. Can she??!!

I've watched a lot of porn on the Internet over the years, a point that was really driven home recently.

About five years ago, my wife and I bought a house in Los Angeles that has a distinct water feature behind it. And a few months ago, I was scrolling through an obscure C-grade porn site when, among the dozens of thumbnails filling the screen, one caught my eye. It appeared to be the water feature from my new backyard.

I clicked on the thumbnail, and there it was: our new house, with four Russians having a very uncircumcised orgy in our water feature. The clip seemed about ten years old and only had a couple thousand views. I had a lot of thoughts in that moment, but the most prevalent was *I did it. I looked at ALL the porn there is on the Internet. It's the only way to explain the statistical improbability of me finding this clip.* The truth is, if you live in a house in Los Angeles, odds are some porn has been shot there, and if you live in a house of any kind anywhere, somebody has definitely fucked in it, so the presence of cameras doesn't really make a difference on a sanitary level. At least I got to see some of the people who fucked in my house before I lived in it. Odds are you didn't. I consider it a gift.

YEARBOOK

I grew up in a perfect-storm-type situation when it comes to being someone who developed a love for weed. I'm from Vancouver, which is and always has been one of the most liberal cities in the world when it comes to weed. Also, I loved hip-hop music, which, aside from a few odd lines here and there, was pretty much telling me to smoke weed all the time. And finally, I was (and still am) a white person, so statistically my odds for really getting in trouble for using it were (and still are) small.

When I was thirteen, I desperately wanted to try it. Yael Folk had tried it with her older brother, and I was so jealous.

ME: What does it feel like?

YAEL FOLK: It burns your throat like crazy.

ME: . . . Awesome.

I had a will but no way. But once I was in high school, the floodgates opened. A few weeks into eighth grade, Steven

Glanzberg, Josh Corber, and Saul Moscovitch came up to me in the hallway.

STEVEN GLANZBERG: **We got some.**

ME: **You got some? Some what?**

SAUL MOSCOVITCH (WHISPERED): **Weed . . .**

Holy shit. It was on.

JOSH CORBER: **After school, we're gonna go to the ravine, and we're gonna smoke it.**

All day, I was freaking out with nervous excitement. I really had no idea what to expect other than a burning throat, and that's probably because being stoned from weed is actually really hard to explain.

We went to the ravine, which is . . . well, a ravine, with a walking path running through the bottom and nice houses along the ridge. It's a few blocks from our high school and seemed like a good place to smoke in an isolated environment, which was generally the goal. We stopped at the 7-Eleven for free Dixie cups of water, which would help combat the inevitable throat burn that we had coming our way. Moscovitch got two cups. When we got there, he pulled out a nug of weed in a small Ziploc bag. It had been in his backpack all day, and because it was particularly fresh and sticky, it had been smushed into a flat little pancake about the size of a nickel.

My only visual experience with weed up till then had been in movies. Cheech and Chong. *Fast Times at Ridgemont High.* *The Breakfast Club* has a weed scene, but I didn't know that until I was around nineteen or twenty. The copy I had as a kid was taped from TV and the weed scene had been cut. Not until years later when I saw the unedited version did I understand that they'd smoked weed, which made the ending with them all being friends make MUCH more fucking sense.

All this is to say that all the portrayals of weed I'd seen were basically giant bags full of dry oregano. Not a tiny bag with a moist little squished nug in it.

ME: What do we do with it?

SAUL MOSCOVITCH: We smoke it.

He reached into his backpack and produced a twelve-inch green plastic bong that he'd bought from a piercing shop downtown. He poured one of his two little cups of water into it and pressed the bud into the bowl. After around thirty attempts, we got the lighting-sucking timing down, and we'd worn away at the nug enough that it actually started burning. I got a big, huge, gigantic hit. I felt the weed's fingers start to tickle their way into my brain and then I exploded in a coughing fit.

"Here." Glanzberg handed me a little water cup. "Have some water. For your throat."

I had some. Then Glanzberg, Corber, and Moscovitch each got one giant rip from the bong before the bowl was cashed.

I was high. Very super-duper high. I remember thinking time was acting funny. One second would take ten seconds; then two seconds, then five seconds would go by in one second, which was a not-normal thing for time to be doing. My vision was processing everything in steps rather than fluid images, as if I were seeing a flipbook of reality. Like I said, I was high. And I was enjoying it—that is, until Moscovitch opened his mouth.

SAUL MOSCOVITCH: Alright. Now we just gotta go back to school so I can stash this bong in my locker, and we're cool.

ME: What?

SAUL MOSCOVITCH: I can't take it home.

ME: Why not?!

SAUL MOSCOVITCH: Because my parents are up my fucking ass ever since I got caught shoplifting that Smashing Pumpkins CD from HMV. They go through my shit all the time. I'm under a fucking microscope, dude! They'll fucking find it.

ME: If you're "under a microscope," why'd you buy a foot-long bong?

SAUL MOSCOVITCH: Because I wanted our first experience to be fucking awesome! Fucking sue me!

ME: Well, we are NOT going back into the school, HIGH, with a stinky bong we just smoked out of!

SAUL MOSCOVITCH: You got any better ideas?

ME: Throw the bong away!

SAUL MOSCOVITCH: Fuck that! This shit cost seventeen dollars! I had to bus downtown to get it. Some dude was getting his cheek pierced in front of me while I was paying. It was fucking gross!

ME: Fine, fine, fine. Let's just be fucking cool and quick.

We walked the three blocks back to school in a manner that was neither fucking cool nor quick. It was a disaster.

I vividly remember Corber—who is now a rabbi—doing the Macarena in the middle of the road as drivers leaned on their horns, trying to vacate this stoned child from traffic. I stopped them at the border of the school's property.

ME: We are NOT going in there!

SAUL MOSCOVITCH: Why not?!

ME: We're gonna get fucking expelled.

SAUL MOSCOVITCH: No we're not. We're just gonna go in there and put it back in my locker.

ME: What if someone sees us?

SAUL MOSCOVITCH: They'll assume we're there for some after-school thing.

ME: What if a teacher asks us why we're there?

SAUL MOSCOVITCH: We'll just say we're there for photography.

ME: What if it's Ms. Correia? She TEACHES photography, dude! Then what?!

SAUL MOSCOVITCH: Then we'll say we're painting sets with stagecraft! Fuck! Chill the fuck out. Don't be a narc.

ME: Don't you dare call me a fucking "narc"!

SAUL MOSCOVITCH: Then don't fucking act like one!

I didn't know much. But I knew goddamn fucking well I didn't want to be a narc. I had no idea what a narc was specifically, but it seemed derogatory as a motherfucker for someone who was (is) desperately trying to be cool.

ME: Fine. Fuck. But be cool and quick. Corber, NO Macarenas. Glanzberg, don't encourage him.

The halls seemed twice as tall as normal. We floated past the auditorium and rounded the corner toward Moscovitch's locker. He opened it, slid open his backpack, and tucked the bong inside the pocket of a snow jacket he had hanging in there. The deed was done. Almost.

"What are you guys doing here?"

We turned to see Mr. Kefalis, which is Greek for "big head," which was hilarious because he had a giant bald head. He was a "cool" teacher, but he would've expelled our asses in a second for having a freshly used foot-long bong in school, mostly because it would be clear we were indeed too stupid for high school if we were doing shit like that. *He* was a narc.

SAUL MOSCOVITCH: Huh?

MR. KEFALIS: What are you guys doing here? School ended forty-five minutes ago.

We looked at each other. We'd practiced for this. It was time.

JOSH CORBER: Photography.

MR. KEFALIS: Where are your cameras?

Holy fuck. This was an intense interrogation. I prayed someone would be able to come up with something.

STEVEN GLANZBERG: In the darkroom.

MR. KEFALIS: . . . Okay.

It was the perfect heist, in a world where the ideal version of a heist was sneaking into school to deposit illegal goods because you had previously been caught stealing a Smashing Pumpkins CD. But either way, we did it. We went to 7-Eleven and got big-ass Slurpees, a tradition that would eventually render me what my doctor calls "pre-diabetic." (But aren't we all?) We wandered around Kerrisdale, and eventually I went home.

As my mom drove me to karate class that night, the weed was wearing off, and I remember thinking, *I would very much like to try that again.* And try it again I did. Pretty much every Friday after school, we would scrounge together whatever money we had and buy a gram of weed.

During the school year, weed was easy to come by. But during summer, shit got much trickier. The dealers wouldn't hang out behind 7-Eleven, because there was no set time when they knew a hundred kids would be there. (This was before cellphones; even pagers were kind of an extravagance.) But Vancouver always had one reliable way to get weed:

Wreck Beach.

The summer after eighth grade had just begun, and I was in a world of shit already. The last day of school, I had bought two ounces of magic mushrooms with the goal of eating them for the first time and selling them to others who would like to eat them for the first time. Don Watkins had an older brother who could get two ounces for a hundred bucks, which I planned to divide up and sell to my friends for ten bucks an eighth, which would essentially give me a free eighth and twenty bucks for my trouble, which everyone deemed acceptable.

We were fucking psyched. During final period, we got our yearbooks, and when the bell rang, everyone rushed into the halls and onto the field to sign each other's shit. "HAGS" (Have A Good Summer) was a popular, if not obligatory, one. But if you were friends with people, the notes got more specific, and if you were me, the notes were specifically a bunch of motherfuckers writing about how psyched they were to do the shrooms I just obtained. ALSO if you were me, you were not the most proactive thinker, so this wouldn't even bump you as it was happening.

I divvied up the shrooms and sold one ounce to Josh Corber and three other dudes I wasn't good friends with. When I got home, I put the second ounce under my bed, tossed my yearbook ON my bed, and took the bus to meet some friends who were smoking weed at one of their grandmas' houses while she was on a cruise. She had one of those chairs that ran up the side of the staircase, and we would take turns riding it while we were baked.

My parents generally didn't snoop through my shit, and flipping through your son's first high school yearbook honestly doesn't seem like an invasion of privacy. I also totally understand that if you were flipping through that yearbook and saw, like, a dozen and a half references to the sale and consumption of hallucinogenic mushrooms, you would then search your kid's room. You would also probably be dumbstruck by how easily you found what you were looking for—an ounce of mushrooms sitting under the bed. *Wow, my son is stupid,* you would think. And you would not be wrong.

That night I came home, and I was in trouble—but not as much as I could have been, due to an odd ally in the form of the Vancouver Police Department.

My parents aren't really drug people, and when they found the shrooms, they were shocked by the quantity. It was a completely full Ziploc bag, essentially the size of a small throw pillow made entirely of fungal hallucinogens. Worried, they called the police to ask about them, because there was no Google and I guess this was their best option—although it seems like some more narc-ass shit to me. But the police told my parents that mushrooms were particularly abundant this time of year and that they were wildly *inex*-pensive, even *free* a lot of the time. This REALLY calmed my parents down. When they sat me down and told me what the cops had said, I jumped all over it.

"Yeah, it's not a big deal; they were free. Someone gave them to me. I didn't do them. I just shoved them under the bed."

"Who gave them to you?"

This was one of those "quick math" situations: Who do I know well enough that he's been around often enough that my parents would know him and would believe he'd gift me a bunch of shrooms but I also dislike enough that I can never really hang out with him again casually because my parents will fucking hate him from here on out? Oddly, the truth worked.

"Don Watkins."

"Hmmm . . . Yeah. I never liked that guy."

Truth be told, I didn't, either. He said anti-Semitic things all the time, so fuck him.

I still got in trouble. Every time I went out, I had to go with a pocket full of quarters, and I had to call my parents from a pay phone every hour on the hour. Which is why the thought of going to Wreck Beach to score weed was scary. It was a forty-five-minute bus ride, which made my phone calls tricky, and once you got there, it was a walk down a five-hundred-step staircase to the beach, which was inhabited by hippies who had been selling weed there since the late seventies. Also, it's a nude beach.

I was terrified.

ME: Have any of you guys been there?

SAUL MOSCOVITCH: Nope. But who cares?

Saul was basically fearless.

ME: Do . . . we have to get naked?

STEVEN GLANZBERG: I don't know. How would they enforce that?

ME: A sign?

STEVEN GLANZBERG: I mean, I don't think they can make you get naked.

ME: What if we're seen as, like, pariahs because we're not naked, and nobody wants to sell us weed because we're clothed, and we went all the way there for nothing!

I was spinning out.

SAUL MOSCOVITCH: Who fucking knows, man? All I know is I wanna smoke weed all summer, and this is the only way I can think of to get it.

We had pooled around fifty bucks. We all had different ways of scrounging cash. In Canada, it was slightly easier because of the one- and two-dollar coins, or "loonies" and "two-nies," which are not doing Canada any favors when it comes to being taken seriously. Every house has little bowls of change scattered around, but in Canada, those bowls could accumulate a decent amount of money. After a few weeks, you could have twenty bucks in change.

I turned to Saul and was like, "Yo, in all honesty, would you get naked for the weed?"

He thought about it. "Yeah, man. I would—would you?"

ME: . . . Yeah. I think I would.

SAUL MOSCOVITCH: Cool.

ME: How do you think it works? Do you think they have cubbies or something where we can put our clothes?

SAUL MOSCOVITCH: I don't know. I imagine they'd have hooks or racks or something.

ME: If we're naked, where do we put the weed once we buy it?

SAUL MOSCOVITCH: I don't know, man! Let's just go!

I called my mom for my hourly check-in, and then we hopped on the bus toward the University of British Columbia, which is right near the beach. We hopped off, I checked in again from a nearby pay phone, and we began the trek down the forested stairs toward the ocean.

I really hope I don't have to take my pants off and have everyone see my dick and my balls and stuff, I remember thinking over and over and over again. We passed a few hippies walking back up the stairs from the beach. *Oh, man, why can't one of these hippies on the stairs sell us weed? That way there would be NO WAY I'd have to have my penis exposed.*

We kept marching until we reached the end of the path, which spilled out onto a beautiful beach. And there we were. Three tweens in skater shorts and Stüssy shirts on a beach with dozens of middle-aged naked people. We stood out like clothed thumbs.

Nudists are weird. My friend went to a nudist colony and came back with a newfound appreciation for clothes. One thing he learned at the colony was that you have to carry around a towel to sit on. Why? So you don't get poop from your sweaty butt on things! Well, fuck me. Let's just wear pants, cool?

"Skunk?!" some guy yelled at us. "You wanna buy some skunk?" It's not a word we had ever used for weed, but we knew what he meant. We went over to a tall, leathery dude who was completely naked except for a fanny pack, which was covering the top two-thirds of his penis, leaving the other third of penis and his testicles dangling below.

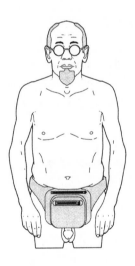

ME: Uh . . . yeah. Hey, sir. We'd like some skunk. We have fifty bucks.

PENIS HIPPIE: Oh shit. More than I thought, okay.

He unzipped his fanny pack and used the lid like a little tabletop, his balls and penis base acting as the legs.

PENIS HIPPIE: Gonna have to combine bags.

He dumped the contents from a few little baggies into one bigger bag, and I was transfixed by his dexterity on this improvised surface and his overall comfort while being naked. I was jealous. My balls had barely seen actual sunlight; they were generally confined to Costco underwear. His looked like those old-timey brown leather baseballs. They seemed like you could strike a match off them. If he did shave them, he did it with a straight razor, no cream. This dude's balls had seen things mine could only dream of. Also, I wondered if this was EXTRA illegal because he was naked and we were fourteen. I can only imagine it wouldn't help his case.

PENIS HIPPIE: Look good to you?

SAUL MOSCOVITCH: Yep! It all looks perfect. We'll take it.

As we walked through the Endowment Lands, the forest surrounding UBC, I had two thoughts:

1. That was totally and a hundred percent worth it, because this is great skunk.

2. It would be so funny if the nude beach was called the Endowment Lands instead of Wreck Beach.

As ninth grade rolled around, we wanted more weed. Like, a lot of it. And by we, I specifically mean me and my friend Brian Baumshtick. Me and Baumshtick didn't come from families with money, as many of our classmates did, and we thought the best way to get some cash was to buy a huge amount of weed at a cheap price, break it up into small portions, and then sell those portions at a profit—a.k.a., become drug dealers. We were telling other kids we were in the market for a bunch of weed, and that's when Billy Yang stepped up.

His father was a hairdresser from Hong Kong and his mother was a British flight attendant and he transferred into our school. I honestly was not that nice to him and we didn't get along that well, but when he came to us saying that he knew these dudes from another school who wanted to unload sixty grams of weed, we were psyched.

BILLY YANG: Sixty grams for three hundred bucks.

ME: What?! How?!

BILLY YANG: Yeah. They wanna get rid of it.

BRIAN BAUMSHTICK: What school do these guys go to?

BILLY YANG: Somewhere east.

ME: Where do we meet them?

BILLY YANG: This weekend, the Crescent.

ME: Perfect.

My parents were out of town, and Danya agreed to drive me and Baumshtick to the Crescent, which is one of Vancouver's richest areas. It's a circular park surrounded by a bunch of mansions. Odd place for a drug deal. It made us a bit scared. Baumshtick came to my house before we left.

BRIAN BAUMSHTICK: We should bring weapons.

ME: What?! I don't know about that.

BRIAN BAUMSHTICK: We totally should! We don't know these guys!

ME: Fine.

I looked around my room and spotted a small souvenir baseball bat that I had gotten from a Seattle Mariners game a few years earlier. "Take this."

"Perfect." Baumshtick swung it around.

I chose my weapon, a pair of wooden nunchucks my dad had gotten me at a flea market. "I'll use these."

We stuffed our weapons in the kangaroo pouches of our hoodies and hopped in the GMC Jimmy, which is a car that was only sold in Canada. My sister pulled up and the dudes were already there. Three big guys who looked about eighteen or nineteen. When you're fourteen, that's fucking terrifying. One of them may have had the beginning of a goatee, which might as well have been a bandolier filled with the severed ears of his enemies. We walked up to the guys while my sister idled nearby.

SCARY DUDE: Yo. You the dudes who's gonna buy this shit?

ME: Uh . . . yeah. We sure are.

SCARY DUDE: You wanna sample it first?

Whoa. Curveball. I'd never been asked if I wanted to sample drugs before. It seemed so professional. I remembered watching *Bad Lieutenant* a few weeks earlier. (We heard there was a lot of nudity, so we rented it. There is, in fact, a lot of nudity. Most of that nudity is of Harvey Keitel, who sports one of the greatest bushes in movie history in that film.) In it, the Bad Lieutenant is always sampling cocaine, rubbing some on his gums to see if it does whatever cocaine is supposed to do when you rub it on your gums. It all of a sudden made me feel quite cool. Even though, as long as it was in fact weed, we were gonna buy it no matter what.

ME: Uh . . . yeah. Sure. We'll sample it.

They pulled out a joint, which they lit and then handed it over to me and Baumshtick. None of them smoked it, which at the time didn't seem that odd. It wasn't until I got more high than I'd ever been that it started to maybe add up a bit. *Perhaps,* I thought, *this weed is laced with something. Maybe*

PCP? Like in the movie Friday. Which was really my only context for this kind of thing.

One of the dudes suddenly changed the tone. "Yo, there's too much heat in this park; we should move this somewhere else."

ME: You can just give it to us.

SCARY DUDE: Nah, we'll meet at the school down the road; it's more isolated there.

They picked the fucking park in the first place, but whatever, we were weed blind and too high to be thinking straight.

ME: Okay.

My sister drove us and dropped us off in front of an elementary school.

SCARY DUDE: Come back here. Around this corner. Nobody will see.

There was absolutely nobody around in the first place, but again, we weren't thinking straight, and even if we were, who knows if we would have done anything different, because we were, at this point in our lives, quite stupid.

They led us around the back of the school to a narrow walkway that dead-ended at some dumpsters. It was indeed very isolated. Then, with a flourish and level of showmanship that I still marvel at to this day, the dudes all reached into a backpack and pulled out gigantic butcher knives. One of them held his up and said proudly, "You motherfuckers are getting *jacked*."

It's a cliché to say that things move in slow motion in these situations, but when you may or may not be on PCP *and* you're in a life-threatening situation, shit gets REAL slow. Molasses slow. Slow enough to have meaningful and in-depth conversations with yourself about all the terrible choices that led to this moment and all the terrible choices you could still make while in it.

My first thought was *Dear god, please don't let Baumshtick pull out that little Seattle Mariners baseball bat.* I did NOT want this to devolve into hand-to-hand combat. They had knives, Baumshtick had a Ken Griffey Jr. souvenir, and I had nunchucks, which, unfortunately, as a weapon, fucking suck. It all seemed so stupid. Why did I even bring these fucking things? They simply didn't work. I had tried to flip them around a few times before, and every time I ended up whacking the fuck out of myself. Even if I did get into a nunchuck groove, as soon as I hit anything, it would send them bouncing all over and fuck up the nunchuck groove or, again, bounce back and whack me in the face.

The next thought I had really made no sense, and my only justification is that PCP makes me rebellious or petulant or something, but I thought, *Fuck these dudes, I'm not giving them SHIT.* They knew we had three hundred bucks on us, but still, I decided to hold my ground.

SCARY DUDE: **Give us your fucking money!**

ME: **No.**

SCARY DUDE: **Give it to us now!**

ME: **. . . No.**

Baumshtick took the opposite approach and unloaded all his belongings instantly. "Here! Take it! Take it all!"

My third and final thought, which was also debatable, was: *We should fucking run.*

Now, Baumshtick was more boxed in than I was, but I guess PCP messes with my spatial awareness, because that didn't seem to matter to me. As the dudes were swinging their knives at us, screaming for us to finish unloading our cash, I leaned into Baumshtick and said, "Run on three. One, two, three." And then I ran. I was ten feet away before Baumshtick even processed what I'd said. Everyone kind of froze, shocked. I stopped in my tracks, looked back at the group. "FUCKING RUN!!"

Baumshtick took off behind me, and the dudes gave chase. We rounded the corner and sprinted across the front lot of the school. My sister saw us coming and started the Jimmy. We hopped in and peeled out, leaving the butcher-knife dudes behind us.

We lived, and I hadn't lost anything, but Baumshtick lost his half of the money and his grandfather's Holocaust necklace.

Pretty much every Jew has some precious heirloom with the word "Holocaust" in front of it. "This is your great-aunt's Holocaust brooch" and "I want you to have Morty's Holocaust watch" are both things that you're very likely to hear in a Jewish household. My assumption is that it means that these particular objects were along for the ride when relatives successfully avoided extermination in the Holocaust, which I guess makes them lucky? It could also make them wildly *un*lucky, depending on how you look at it.

BRIAN BAUMSHTICK: My mom is gonna notice it's gone. I'm fucking DEAD.

We came to school on Monday a bit traumatized. Billy Yang commiserated with us: "I can't believe they fucking did that!" We thought he mmmmaybe set us up, but that would be a fucked-up thing to do. I mean, we could have fucking died. He swore he didn't, and to help make it up to us, he said he'd reach out to the guys to try to get the Holocaust necklace back.

A few days later, he told us they'd sell it back to us for a hundred fifty bucks. Since I didn't give up my money in the robbery, I offered to pay for it, but we ended up splitting it. Billy Yang took our money and got the guys to sell him the necklace back, which he returned to us by the end of the week. We were ultimately grateful but also fucked up from the whole thing. It was traumatic, and it made us nervous when we were walking home from school for years to come. And the worst part was, we were never really sure if we were set up or not.

Until around fifteen years later.

I got a call from Baumshtick.

BRIAN BAUMSHTICK: You'll never fucking guess what just happened. I'm at a party and guess who comes up to me? Billy fucking Yang!

ME: Holy FUCK! What did he say?

BRIAN BAUMSHTICK: He said that he set us up.

ME: Really?

BRIAN BAUMSHTICK: Yeah. AND that it was the worst thing he's ever done and that he's felt bad about it for the last fifteen years. He apologized. I accepted. He asked me to apologize to you, too.

I had really not been expecting this, nor was I expecting how much closure it would give me. It also gave me context as to why it all happened in the first place: I wasn't that nice to Billy Yang. And since he was tiny and I was big, he got back at me the only way he thought he could—by tricking me into getting robbed by even bigger dudes. We didn't just get randomly robbed; we were dicks to a dude who was a lot angrier than we thought he was, and he got back at us.

If it was a movie, we'd be the big dumb bullies, and he'd be the clever little kid who got revenge by using his brain. Maybe we were the villains of the story and Billy Yang was the hero? I don't know. Those butcher knives were pretty big. I guess we'll call it even.

Also, if weed was legal, none of that shit would have happened in the first place. Well, maybe it would have, because we were actually too young to buy legal weed. But still. You'd think legality brings with it less danger. I don't know anyone who's been robbed at knifepoint trying to buy some Mike's Hard Lemonade.

Either way, it's legal in Canada now and, at the time of this writing, inching slowly toward legalization in America, but there's still a long way to go, probably because it's just too effective a way to persecute minorities and keep prisons full, which are things that they love to do in America.

I used to think a lot about why I smoked weed, but, honestly, I stopped. Because I realized the only reason I was thinking about it was because of the negative stigma, and the only reason it has a negative stigma is that it makes it easier for white people to control nonwhite people, which unfortunately is also the reason for a shitload of other things.

There's stuff that makes our lives better that hasn't been stigmatized, and nobody gives those things a second thought. Nobody thinks about why they have a strong desire to wear shoes. Nobody says that people who wear shoes are denying reality. Instead, the consensus on shoes is that we use them to adapt to reality. If we don't wear them, our feet will hurt. They make our journey more comfortable, and we don't judge ourselves for wearing them. They don't make walking any less "real." Nobody's ever like, "You're not really experiencing walking. You're under the fog of footwear." They're like, "Yeah. Our feet aren't made for walking in the environments we've settled in as a species. Wear shoes."

That's why I smoke weed. It's additive to my journey. It makes getting from here to there manageable and comfortable.

There's this odd concept of functionality that people apply to some things but not others. Our feet need cushioning. Our skin needs protecting. Our muscles need exercise. Our asses need wiping. But our brains? Don't touch those! They're perfect, and if you're having a hard time with yours and are smoking weed, it's bad! Unfortunately, as well designed as people are, we just aren't completely cut out for this world we live in. We need shoes, sunblock, exercise, toilet paper—and weed.

People criticize weed for changing your view of reality. But sunglasses *literally* change your view of reality, and nobody gives them a hard time for it.

Weed is my sunglasses. Weed is my shoes. I'm not quite cut out for this world, but weed makes it okay.

THE MOHEL

I had started doing stand-up when I was thirteen, and by the time I was fourteen, I was getting better at it. I wasn't fantastic, but I was probably on the better end of the spectrum of the comics in Vancouver at the time. Coupled with the fact that I was a teenager, I was a bit of a novelty. Like when you see one of those YouTube videos of an elephant that can paint: They're usually not that great at painting, but the fact that it's an elephant really buys it some points.

I was at the Urban Well, which was a bar that had weekly stand-up shows on Tuesday nights, where I performed regularly. They would also let me hang out after my sets, which was technically illegal. As a young stand-up, that was always part of the challenge; a lot of bars weren't really clear on the legality of the whole thing, which I get, because it probably didn't come up that often. But, in a bizarre stroke of luck, right after I turned fourteen, I performed at a charity show where the premier (kind of like the governor) of British Columbia happened to be. My mom, who was at pretty much every stand-up show I ever did—half out of love and support, and half out of the fact that I couldn't drive and needed a lift to and from the shows—marched up to the premier and explained the problem we were having. He told us that technically it *was* legal for me to perform at a club or bar, as long as I was backstage before my performance and left immediately after. We even got his office to print out the bylaw and mail it to us, and we would carry it around and show it to the owners of the bars and clubs if they hesitated to let me perform.

The Urban Well didn't give a shit about any of that and just let me hang out. Which was fucking fantastic. Because as a fourteen-year-old, being in a bar, even one your mom is at, is exciting. Also, the stand-up comics were WAY nicer to me than they had any obligation to be. As a thirty-nine-year-old man, the concept of chilling with a fourteen-year-old stand-up comic is fucking insane: I would literally NEVER do it. It just seems strange to me. But, bless them, these comics would let me sit at the big kids' table while they said some truly horrific shit that was so thrilling to hear adults say.

So I did a set and was talking to some of the other comedians afterward, when a guy in a suit came up to me and asked if we could chat. I remember thinking that maybe he was an agent or a manager who liked my jokes and wanted to send me out on auditions. He had that sort of vibe. Kind of slick, cool, and maybe even a bit . . . flashy. I'm not gonna say douchey, but I clearly thought it enough to say that I wasn't gonna say it, so it was for sure in the mix. I was like, "Yeah, sure, let's talk, dude."

We sat down and he told me that he loved my material and was actually looking for someone he could pay to write some jokes for him. He said to call him if I was interested, and then, before leaving, he gave me his card. It read:

Dr. Stephen Bredeson, Mohel

Now, if you're not familiar with the term, a mohel is the dude who, in Jewish tradition, performs circumcisions on our sweet, unsuspecting, eight-day-old male babies. This was, quite honestly, pretty fucking confusing to me. My mind flooded with questions. Did he want mohel jokes? Was he giving a speech or a toast at a wedding or something? Was the whole mohel thing, like, a day job, and he secretly wanted to be a comedian, so he approached an okay teenage comic to write his material for him? Material, I remember thinking, that would probably have to be about the life of a middle-aged, flashy, maybe douchey mohel in order to feel organic coming out of his mouth. That was a challenging prospect, considering most of my time was spent listening to Wu-Tang Clan, smoking weed, and playing GoldenEye on Nintendo 64.

The next day, I called the dude. He told me that the jokes were in fact to be used IN his mohel ceremony, or service, whatever it's called . . . the thing where they cut the baby's dick tip off. One question was answered, but many more fell into its place. *Is that even a good idea?* I remember thinking. *Like, a funny mohel? Do people want that? This dude is dealing with your baby's penis. Do you want him cracking jokes?*

I'd probably want the guy slicing the tip of my baby's dick off to be quite serious about it. No horseplay. No nonsense. "I cut babies' dicks and I don't fuck around about it." That would probably be the attitude I would want. Also, what if the jokes didn't play? Then you're having your newborn's tiny baby dick circumcised by a guy who's up there swinging and missing comedically. Nothing makes you doubt someone more than seeing them bomb. That would be potentially horrifying for a parent.

He explained that he thought the jokes could be good ice-breakers throughout the service. "People are nervous," he said, "and it might be nice to break the tension with some jokes." I was like, "Oh yeah, of course. That would be really nice." I should add that I had never attended a circumcision in my life and truly had no fucking clue what the vibe was like, but I kept that to myself. He said he would pay me fifty bucks a joke, and we planned to meet the following week to go over what I had written.

Here's the thing: I needed money. I had none. I never got, like, a formal allowance. My parents would give me money to get specific things when I needed them; I wasn't going to school in a burlap sack or anything, but I didn't have, like, savings. Which was fine, until I started smoking weed.

Now, weed was cheap back then. When I first smoked it at the beginning of eighth grade, it was fifteen bucks a gram. Then, I think due to competition, it dropped to ten bucks. This was game-changing. Because all you needed was three people to come up with around three bucks each. Three people put in for a gram, you roll two fat-ass joints, and you're all getting nice and baked for the price of a Big Mac.

This payment system the mohel was proposing was kinda vague and, for that reason, awesome. No matter what, I could write ten jokes, so I said, "Yeah. Let's do this."

For the next week after school, as I watched *Star Trek: The Next Generation,* I wrote mohel jokes. These are some of the actual jokes:

- He is gonna be the coolest dude in preschool. How many kids his age can say they've survived a knife fight?

- I used to work in Winnipeg, but I had to move to Vancouver. You see, there's not a lot of work for a mohel who shivers uncontrollably. (This is a VERY Canadian joke.)

- Please give it up for our musical act, the Slice Girls!

- Now, just give me a moment as I oil up the chainsaw.

- (Before putting wine on the baby's lips, which is part of the service:) Excuse me, sir, can I see some ID? Just kidding, he for sure looks old enough.

- He's not driving home, is he?

- The only problem with being a mohel is that you get used to the ceremony. Last night, I found myself going through a half-hour service before I could cut a carrot for my salad.

At the end of the week, I called to tell him I had a good batch and asked how I should get the jokes to him. He told me he would pick me up after school on Monday and we'd go to a nearby coffee shop to go over them.

It was raining that Monday, and I was standing with Fogell and Evan outside 7-Eleven, which is a statement that applies to about 90 percent of my life between the ages of thirteen and seventeen. I was bragging that I was getting money for writing these jokes, and my friends were, by all accounts, quite jealous, which thrilled me. And to make things even better, at that moment, the mohel pulled into the

7-Eleven parking lot in, I shit you not, a fucking Ferrari. Like, a brand-new incredible Ferrari. The kind that, if you're in high school, is simply the dopest shit you could ever imagine. The kids in the parking lot looked at it like a spaceship was landing. "What is this thing doing here? Where did it come from? What does it want?"

I was psyched. I turned back to my friends to soak in the last bit of envy and admiration, but . . . their faces did not look envious. Instead, they looked horrified.

I was like, "What?"

Sammy Fogell turned to me. "Don't get in that car."

ME: Why the fuck not?

SAMMY FOGELL: Do I have to say it?

ME: What?

SAMMY FOGELL: He's gonna try to fuck you!

ME: What?! You're crazy! No he's not!

SAMMY FOGELL: Yes! He will!

ME: He's a fucking doctor!

SAMMY FOGELL: Who SPECIFICALLY specializes in little kids' dicks! What kind of person does that? I'll tell you what kind! The kind who LOVES little kids' dicks. The kind who chose a life and profession that is BASED on the touching of little kids' dicks!

Shit. He had a point. I struggled for high ground.

ME: Well, he slices up their dicks! If he loved their dicks so much, why is he slicing them up? He hates little-kid dicks. He's the last guy to want to fuck a kid.

"No, man." Fogell stared into my eyes. "Dude is circumcising the dicks. Making them look nicer, prettier, cleaner. That dude is gussying up those little-kid dicks. That dude LOVES little-kid dicks. He's got a flashy car, which little kids like. He needs jokes and he could have hired ANYONE, and instead he hires, what? A little fucking kid with a little-fucking-kid dick."

Fuck. I couldn't deny it. I was in fact a little fucking kid and I did in fact have a little-fucking-kid dick. The mohel looked over at me and honked the horn. I looked back at my friends.

ME: Dudes, this motherfucker is gonna give me five hundred bucks. If he fucks me, it'll almost be worth it. I'm doing this shit.

I walked over and got in the car like I was in the opening scene of *Mystic River*. As we drove away, I looked back at my friends through the tiny, impractical rear window of the Ferrari. They waved meekly, as if to say, "Nice knowing you. Or at least this version of you."

The guy didn't try to fuck me. Instead, he took me to a coffee shop, and I presented him with the handwritten list of jokes, at which time, ironically, he seemed to feel *I* was fucking *him*.

He looked them over, scowling.

I got nervous.

ME: So . . . uh . . . I wrote ten jokes; at fifty bucks a joke, that's five hundred bucks.

He put down the paper.

MOHEL: I'm not sure I like all these jokes. What's this "Slice Girls" one even mean?

ME: Oh! It's a reference to the Spice Girls! They're super-popular. People will love it.

MOHEL: Do I gesture after I say it? Like they're gonna come out?

ME: Sure! That could be funny! Gesture! Then say, "Just kidding!"

(Note: No good joke requires the words "just kidding" at the end of it.)

MOHEL: I'm just not sure all these are gonna work. Can I just pay you for the ones that I like?

Fuck. I hadn't accounted for this. I was already out of my element, and now I had to negotiate my own rate? Again, at this point, the extent of my monetary knowledge was loonies and grams. I tried to stand my ground.

ME: Uh . . . no. That doesn't really work for me. Like . . . I could have worked all week and if you only happened to like one joke, then I only get fifty bucks. That wasn't the deal. I don't think I would have agreed to that.

He didn't seem thrilled, but at this point what the fuck was he gonna do? It's weird enough that he hired a kid to do his writing for him; it would be straight up sociopathic to then not pay that kid what you promised him. He didn't have enough cash on him. I think he was only expecting to have to give me like two hundred dollars or something. But I wasn't gonna waste this opportunity, and the Ferrari was not helping his case.

ME: You're driving me home anyway. Maybe we can just stop at an ATM.

We did and he paid me. When he dropped me off at home, I watched him drive off and didn't feel great. I wished he was happier with the transaction. But the truth was, I thought they were pretty good jokes and I really wouldn't have handed them in if I didn't. After all, for all I knew he could have been an amazing conduit to a whole world of medical professionals who needed jokes. Surgeons, anesthesiologists. Man, I could have written two thousand proctologist jokes in an afternoon. But it didn't seem like I'd be getting that recommendation.

I remember thinking, *He's never gonna use them.* Which kind of made me sad, but I tried to make myself feel better: *It's fine. I got five hundred bucks.* Five hundred bucks that I would eventually use a portion of to buy two ounces of mushrooms, one ounce of which my parents would find under my bed and throw in the garbage, which would make me even sadder.

I also remember saying to myself: *Hey, just 'cause you write something doesn't mean anyone has to see it or hear it. It still exists just as much as anything else does, which is pretty fleeting.*

That didn't make me feel as good as the money thing did. Not because I like money, although I do, as it makes everything easier, but because I had been paid to write. It was possible. It had happened, and I was determined to make it happen again. And maybe the next time, the person would be super-psyched with what I was giving them. Not just like, "Do I have to pay for all of this?" but instead like, "This shit is fucking dope! Can I pay you even *more* than I said I would?" (This has yet to happen.)

Anyway, it gave me hope, which is what I needed to chase something I really wanted. How much did I want it? I'll tell you exactly how much: enough to get in a Ferrari alone with a dude who made it his business to ensure the aesthetic superiority of *very* young people's penises. That's how much.

☙ ☙ ☙

Twenty-two years later, I got a call from my mother, who had just been at a wedding in Vancouver, and who was sitting at her table? The mohel. He continues to circumcise the Jewish youth of the lower mainland to this very day.

"Guess what?" Mom said. "He still tells your jokes."

AN EVENING AT
THE IMPROV

As I was going into tenth grade, I had yet to have a girl-friend of any type, which was a bit of a bummer. I think I was probably just wayyyy too scared and nervous. And there are probably a lot of reasons for that, but one thing I've grown to appreciate is just how much the first porn I saw spooked me.

It was called *The Fisherman's Wife,* and someone had given it to me on VHS. I had never seen actual sex of any type and I was NOT fucking prepared for it. It was dirty. Not entry-level porn. (I apologize for the following description, and I'll try to make it as not gross as possible.)

It started in a bait shop, where the bait saleswoman and a customer had sex on the counter. They had sex in various standing positions, and then, when it was time for the gentleman to finish, he did so into the tip jar and then kinda tossed the contents on the lady as she happily rubbed it on herself.

Again, I was NOT fucking prepared. This is what sex was? It was so much more graphic than I thought it would be. I have to stand while doing it? Do I keep my fishing boots on like the guy in the video did? Who brings the tip jar? Do I? Does the lady?

It scared me. If the first time you went skiing, someone sent you down a black-diamond run and then tossed a cup of jizz at you, you'd probably be a bit scared to hit the slopes from there on out. (I'm not great at analogies.) Also, I was NOT psyched about my body. I remember watching *The Sopranos* and noting that Tony kept his undershirt on while having sex. *Awesome,* I thought. *If he can do that, so can I.*

I had a huge crush on a girl named Moira. We were partners in cooking class, which was basically wall-to-wall conversation, and we seemed to hit it off. Every class was like a little date. A taste of what it would be like if we were a couple who loved to make lemon meringue pie all the time. I REALLY liked her. And finally, one day . . . I heard she liked me back. Like *like* liked me back.

That weekend there was a party at Dan Vertlieb's house, and I went up to her in the kitchen and asked, "Will you go out with me?" She said yes. I was fucking THRILLED.

Monday was the greatest day of my life. I couldn't wait to get to school to see her. We baked a strudel, and at the end of class we kissed on the lips.

I was fucking soaring.

As soon as I saw Moira on Tuesday, I knew shit was fucked.

Moira: Hey, Seth . . .

Me: Hey! Everything okay?

Moira: Uh . . .

Oh no.

Moira: I think I liked it better when we were just friends.

There's this episode of *The Simpsons* where Lisa Simpson dumps Ralph Wiggum on television and Bart is able to pinpoint the moment where Ralph's heart breaks. I always related to this moment on a deep, deep level.

I told her I also liked it better when we were friends, which seemed like the least humiliating thing to say at the moment. We hugged and went our separate ways.

That night, I did stand-up and bombed, which is not surprising considering my two big jokes were:

1. Krazy Glue—what's so crazy about it? It sticks to things really well. That's not crazy! That's exactly what it's supposed to do! It's the most logical glue on the market! Why are we stigmatizing it?!

2. It must have been really exciting for a lot of people when sumo wrestling was invented. Because one day you were just a fat guy in a diaper, and then, all of a sudden, BAM, you're a *sumo wrestler*. Which is so much better. "What do you do?" "Oh, me? I'm a fat guy in a diaper." "Really? I met a similar guy, but he had a MUCH better job description."

I had gotten a manager in L.A. through a road comic I'd met at Yuk Yuk's one night. His name was Ray Saperstein and he was pretty fucking weird; I ultimately had to fire him, and it sucked. (Page 96.)

Ray got me a spot to audition for Just for Laughs, which was Canada's biggest comedy festival. Ironically, the audition was in Los Angeles at a showcase at the Improv on Melrose. I had grown up watching *An Evening at the Improv,* and it was probably one of the reasons I wanted to do stand-up in the first place. My parents packed up the car and we drove to L.A. for the weekend.

The showcase was early, at like 6 P.M. I remember thinking, *Man, it's strange doing stand-up when the sun's still out.* The Improv was about half-full of tourists and day drinkers who'd lost track of the time. My spot was approaching, and I paced around the back of the club. Then Ray came up to me.

RAY: Hey. You were supposed to be next, but Jerry Seinfeld is dropping in. You're gonna go on after.

It was 1998. *Seinfeld* was in its final season and was the biggest comedic cultural sensation on earth. This was a fucking disaster.

ME: I have to go on AFTER?

RAY: Yeah.

ME: Can I go on before?

RAY: Nope.

ME: Why not?

RAY: Because he's gonna be here any second and they don't want to make him wait for you to finish before he goes up!

ME: But this guy's just finishing and he's not here yet.

Ray motioned to the entrance, where, through a window, I saw a vintage Porsche pull up. Jerry Seinfeld stepped out and walked through the front door.

RAY: He's here. You're up after.

ME: Isn't that bad?!

RAY: It could be good! He'll warm 'em up for you!

ME: They won't want me after that! They'll be done! They'll be so warm, they'll be cooked! They'll be done!

RAY: Or they'll be begging for more!

Jerry sauntered through the club and, without breaking

his stride, walked up onstage just as his introduction finished. The small crowd went BERSERK. He was preparing
for his special *I'm Telling You for the Last Time,* which is basically him telling all his best, most famous jokes. He annihi-
lated to a degree I didn't really realize was possible, and I
stood in the back hoping a light would fall and cave his head
in. I was enraged. I remember thinking, *This motherfucker.
How dare he? This is a fucking showcase for amateurs to secure
a spot at a Canadian comedy festival, and he's just going to show
up and slap his ten-foot dick on the table and fuck everyone else
into oblivion?*

He left the stage, and you could sense the shock in the
audience as the emcee started to introduce me. They were
like, "Really? More? We're good. Nothing will top that. Let's
call it an early evening."

I took the stage to a skeptical smattering of applause,
which I totally understand. Again, if someone told me I had
to watch a sixteen-year-old do stand-up, I'd be skeptical, too.

What followed was disastrous. My first joke was about bicycle cops; Vancouver had just dispatched a squad of them
in an attempt to be environmentally conscious.

"Bicycle cops seem like a good idea, but what if someone
commits a crime on top of a big hill?"

To say nobody laughed would be an understatement. It
felt like they were taking away laughs I had previously gotten. It was negative-laughter. I later learned they didn't have
bicycle cops in L.A., and as such, the joke was nonsense.

I never recovered. To this day, I remember standing on
the stage, the crowd so quiet that I could hear the electric
hum of the speakers, and thinking, *That's not good!*

I didn't get into the festival, and all the comics back in

Vancouver knew it. The next week I was at a club and had just come offstage when a comic named Darryl Lenox came up to me.

DARRYL: Look, I'm just gonna be honest with you, Seth. Why the fuck are you telling jokes about Krazy Glue and bicycle cops, man?

ME: What do you mean?

DARRYL: I mean you're sixteen years old! Talk about sixteen-year-old shit! Anyone can talk about glue and bikes and shit. Talk about shit only you can talk about! Like, what do you do on weekends?

ME: Uh . . . try to buy beer and sneak into strip clubs?

DARRYL: Write about THAT! You got a girlfriend?

ME: No. I wish. I had one, but I got dumped after three days.

Darryl burst out laughing. "Write about THAT!"

I did. It was a so-so joke about how short my only relationship was: "Three days! That's it! It won't leave us much to reminisce about if we run into each other on the street in a few years. 'Hey! Good to see you! Yeah, those were good times. Remember . . . uh . . . Thursday? Thursday was good. Not as good as Wednesday. But better than Friday.'"

It was the first time I turned real anguish into comedy, and I was proud of it. Probably way too proud. So proud I didn't really take the time to look at it from Moira's perspective. It eventually got back to her that I was telling a joke about her, and she always said it was fine, but what the fuck else was she gonna say?

When *Superbad* was gearing up to get made, me and Evan wanted to name all the characters after our actual friends from high school and, when possible, match them up to real stories that happened. Everyone cleared their name for use in the film—except Moira.

For a long time, because I'm a dumbass, I was pissed. And also confused. Why wouldn't she want her name in the movie?

But now I'm like: Of course she didn't want her name in the fucking movie. She'd already been the subject of one of my dumb jokes on a small scale, and I'm SURE she didn't love it. Then, years later, I approach her and am like: "Remember how I used to tell that joke about you and you probably really didn't like it? Well, now I want to put it in a big Hollywood movie." All this poor girl did was date me for three days. She didn't sign up to be the subject of my stupid writing for . . . OH NO, I'M STILL DOING IT.

(For the purposes of this book, Moira's name was changed.)

FIRING RAY

he first time I had to fire an adult, I was eighteen years old.

I had been living in L.A. for about a year, and Ray Saperstein was still my manager. "What the fuck is a manager, anyway?" is a question that I'm sure many people have, and the truth is, it's a tough one to answer. They help you get work, guide your career, connect you to other people who could help you achieve your goals, and if you're Ray Saperstein, they generally humiliate you and really make you question why you chose this person to represent you, both figuratively and literally.

The reason for that was actually simple: He was the only person who would do it. A failed stand-up comedian, he started representing other stand-up comics in the eighties. Some of them were really good. Some were okay. Most of them were not that okay. I was somewhere in the middle. He had an office in L.A. and was willing to be my manager, so I went with it.

Ray was a BIG dude. Maybe six foot four and 240 pounds. There was a twenty-four-year age difference between us, which right away was awkward, because technically he worked for me. I paid him. And he basically just yelled at me constantly for not having a fax machine. It was a lot for a teenager to wrap his head around.

I started to NOT like him pretty quickly. The way he interacted with people, his taste, his vision for my future, his boundaries (he asked me to move into his house, which is objectively insane and, in retrospect, wildly creepy). He once took me to Las Vegas because he demanded I see Emo Philips live, which was fun but not something a seventeen-year-old would really choose to do. And he kept demanding we go back to see Carrot Top, who he insisted was "wayyyy funnier than you'd think! And his control of the crowd is unheard of! You GOTTA see Top live." He called him "Top" as though he was name-dropping "Clooney."

"I was talking to Top the other day . . ." Then he'd coyly lean in. "Carrot . . . Anyway, Top was like, 'I got this new bit with a megaphone made of cheese . . .' "

I knew I had to part ways.

I had just bought my first car, an Acura that would later get destroyed on my first date with my wife. (Page 129.) *Freaks and Geeks* had been canceled, and I was unemployed. Ray was pestering me about a recent decision I had made to not be the third banana on what seemed to me like a terrible Warner Bros. sitcom that revolved around Nikki Cox, who was one of the stars of *Unhappily Ever After,* which itself was a terrible sitcom that was a rip-off of *Married . . . with Children,* yet another terrible sitcom.

"Take the gig!! She's a star!!"

I told him we should have lunch to talk about it.

Ray had suggested some giant fancy lunch spot on La Brea, and I pulled up in my brand-new (certified pre-owned) Acura 3.2 TL, which, according to the dealer, was sporty with ample trunk space. When I walked in, I was super fucking nervous, but I had a game plan: Fire him right away, don't order food or drinks, do it nicely and quickly, then go. I figured we'd be in a busy upscale restaurant with tons of his industry peers around, so he'd be polite and the whole thing would be cool as fuck.

I sat down with Ray, who was waiting for me at a table for two smack in the middle of the place, and shit went haywire right off the bat.

Before I could even say "hi," the waiter appeared. "Can I get you guys anything?"

I said, "Uh . . . maybe come back in a sec—"

Ray instantly interrupted, which he loved to do. "The tortilla soup here is amazing! Two tortilla soups!"

WAITER: I'll bring those right out!

RAY: I can't wait for you to try this soup! It's amazing! Did you get a car?

ME: Uh . . . look . . . before we get too into this . . . I have something I need to say.

His face changed. He knew what was coming.

RAY: Go ahead.

ME: So . . . yeah . . . I appreciate the effort you've put in for me, but . . . I think it's time I find another manager.

RAY: Why?

ME: Well . . . I . . . just think that—

WAITER: Here are your tortilla soups! Be careful—they're hot!

The waiter plopped the soups down in front of us. "Fresh cotija cheese?"

ME: Uh . . . I'm good. Ray?

He was just staring at me. I noticed his fists were clenched tightly.

ME: I think we're both good.

The waiter left, and Ray just kept staring.

RAY: Why?

ME: Uh . . . well . . . you haven't actually gotten me any work at all. . . .

RAY: I've tried! It's not my fault! And I DID get you one job and YOU don't want it! I'm telling you, Nikki Cox is a STAR!

He was getting loud. People were staring. The whole plan was going to fucking shit.

ME: Look, man . . . just relax. . . .

RAY: Do you know how hard I've worked for you? And how hard it is to deal with your fucking parents?

Whoa. Now, as an eighteen-year-old, I wasn't exactly used to being put in a position to *defend* my parents.

ME: Uh . . . I think my parents have actually been pretty chill. . . .

RAY: They wouldn't let you move in with me.

ME: I didn't want to move in with you!

RAY: Why not?!

ME: I just turned eighteen and moved out from living with my parents! I don't wanna be roommates with a forty-five-year-old man!

RAY: I'm forty-two!

(Which seemed like a crazy distinction to make at the time, but as I get older, I get it.)

I knew I just had to end it.

ME: Look, dude. I'm sorry. But this is it. It's over. I appreciate the soup and your time. But we're not working together anymore.

I got up to leave.

He threw some cash on the table and followed me out the front door, calling after me: "Wait! Seth . . . come to my car."

ME: What?

RAY: Come to my car.

ME: Why?

RAY: . . . I have a surprise.

Jesus.

ME: I'm not gonna go to your fucking car, dude.

RAY: Why not?

ME: I just don't want to. I'm afraid you're gonna fucking kill me, man.

RAY: I'm not gonna kill you!

ME: Of course you'd say that!

RAY: Just come to my car. Don't worry.

ME: When you say, "Don't worry," it makes it fucking worse, man!

RAY: I'm parked right there!

He pointed halfway up the block. "Just come to my fucking car!"

It felt like one of the stupider things I'd ever done, but I was like, "Fine."

We walked in silence up the block together, and I remember thinking there was maybe a 45 percent chance he was going to murder me. When we got to his car, he angrily opened his trunk, reached in, and pulled out a gigantic printer/fax machine and SHOVED it into my arms. I could barely hold it.

He stared me dead in my eyes.

"Happy birthday."

Then he hopped in his car and sped off up La Brea.

I lugged the printer/fax back to my new car and was thrilled that I hadn't been murdered, and to find that the dealer's promise of ample trunk room wasn't a lie.

AMSTERDAM

When I called my parents and told them I was meeting my friend Ben in Europe, they were nervous. Me and Ben had been best friends since we were ten years old and met at summer camp. I had never really traveled alone before, but I was nineteen and living in Los Angeles by myself, so it seemed like I could handle it.

DAD: **Where are you going?**

ME: **Amsterdam and then Paris.**

MOM: **You're just going to do drugs.**

ME: **No. We're also going to Paris.**

DAD: **Where are you staying?**

ME: **Youth hostels.**

MOM: **You're gonna get robbed.**

ME: **No I'm not.**

MOM: **Yes you are. Youth hostels are VERY dangerous. You have to wear a money belt and keep your passport and money in the money belt.**

ME: Fine! I'll wear a money belt.

MOM: Okay. As long as you wear a money belt.

I didn't know what the fuck a money belt was, and I was not at all psyched when I found out. It's kind of like a flat fanny pack that, I think in theory, is supposed to fit seamlessly between your pants and underpants, resting in the area that for me is under my tummy and above the base of my penis, which I believe is called the *mons pubis,* but I'm not sure.

Unfortunately for the paranoid traveler, the money belt is actually too big to fit under your waistband, so it sticks up, like, four inches above it, while the thin elastic belt wraps around your love handles, doing a bad job of keeping the whole deal in place. It's a fucking nightmare, but I promised I'd wear one.

I got my plane ticket and was excited to fly KLM, which, of course, stands for Royal Dutch Airlines. The trip got off to a rocky start, as I found myself in a middle seat in coach for what was an eleven-hour flight. I'd brought nothing to read or watch, because I was nineteen and it didn't even remotely occur to me. I had nothing but discomfort to keep me occupied. At one point, I wrapped my blanket around my head and tried to mentally disconnect my brain from my body. This resulted in me weeping openly and loudly for about fifteen minutes as the people on either side of me completely ignored me, which is again one of those things I look back on and think, *That's kind of fucked up.* I probably would have asked what was wrong, but I guess everyone's afraid of getting into conversations on airplanes. As I've gotten older, I'd rather be seated next to a feral wolf than some producer I kinda know who wants to chat. At least the wolf won't say gross sexual things assuming that I'll think they're cool.

I arrived at the Amsterdam Airport Schiphol at around 11 A.M. I was supposed to meet my friend Ben at the Vondel-park at 3 P.M., so that we could then go and check in to our hostel together. Now, I guess it's important to note that nei-ther of us had a cellphone that worked in Europe, because I'm not even sure that shit existed back then. We just made a plan and were supposed to do it, which seems reckless and terrifying in retrospect. These days, I text my wife while I'm in line for popcorn at the theater to make sure the seat-finding process is going okay. The fact that I flew to a differ-ent continent and was just supposed to meet my friend at a certain place at a certain time feels like something out of the Middle Ages. It's like when you hear that NASA sent people to the moon with a scientific calculator; that's what meeting someone without a cellphone seems like to me now.

I found a train, made it to the city, and walked toward the park with my gigantic backpack strapped to my sweaty back, making it to the downtown area by, like, 1:30 P.M. I had some time to kill, so I headed to a small, dark Moroccan weed café.

This was my first time buying weed in a legal setting, and when you're me, that's something you never forget. It's a fucking dream come true. The normalization of something you've been told your whole life is highly illicit was oddly validating. Also, I was a HUGE *Pulp Fiction* fan, which was probably most Americans' first introduction to how those weed cafés worked. And it blew my fucking mind.

"I'll take a gram of your strongest marijuana, please."

It felt fantastic to say.

I wish I could say the smoking of it went as well.

Now, I grew up smoking very good weed in British Co-lumbia, but this was next-level shit. I felt like the monkey touching that obelisk in *2001*. It was the future. And my brain was NOT ready for it. I took a few hits too many, all the while not knowing what to do with my giant backpack. It was like having a legless, armless person to deal with. Awkward, big. Like the opposite of one of those inflatable clowns that pop back up no matter how much you punch them. No matter what I did, I couldn't get this fucking thing to stand up and not take up the same space an unconscious child would. I bet in actuality it was bothering nobody and I just looked like a super-stoned dude who couldn't stop trying to balance an impossible-to-balance backpack, but it didn't feel like that. There were real stakes.

By the time I finally finished my way-too-strong joint, it was time to go meet Ben. I found my way back to the park, and sure enough, there he was. Astronauts made it to the moon, and I found Ben in Amsterdam. We checked in to the hostel, which, if you haven't stayed in one, is a fucking odd environment. There was a bizarre mix of young stoners and slightly older people who don't have a lot of money and just want to have sex with tons of prostitutes.

The first night in the hostel was very awkward. The funny thing was that we never actually saw any of the ten people we were sharing the room with, because we were always in bed before they got back and somehow still managed to sleep later than all of them. Nonetheless, the first night, we were awoken by one of our nameless, faceless roommates shuffling around in the dark. He loudly flopped onto a bed, waking up everyone, then spoke in an American-sounding accent at full volume: "Hey."

Nobody responded, because nobody knew who he was talking to.

"Hey," he said again.

Silence.

"Hey, man. Above me. I'm talking to you."

Thank fucking god it wasn't me. I was safely on a bottom bunk, out of the path of this freight train of awkwardness. A very quiet, very nervous, French-sounding voice responded.

"'Ello. Oui. Are you talking to me?"

"Yeah, man."

The whole thing was playing out like a radio show in the pitch-black room. I even cast it in my head. The American guy was kind of a strung-out Vincent Kartheiser–looking dude, and because I'm dumb, the French guy was wearing a striped shirt and a beret and had a pencil mustache and a stuffed animal that looked like a baguette with googly eyes.

FRENCH GUY: Umm . . . 'ow can I 'elp you? (He clutched his baguette doll tightly.)

VINNIE K–LOOKING AMERICAN: You took my bed.

FRENCH GUY: I deed what?

VINNIE K–LOOKING AMERICAN: You took my bed, man. It's fine, because I got another one, but I just want you to know that you took my bed and I know you took my bed.

FRENCH GUY: I took your bed? I am very sorry, I deedn't realize.

VINNIE K–LOOKING AMERICAN: What do you mean? My stuff was on it.

FRENCH GUY: Eet was? Maybe I didn't see eet?

VINNIE K–LOOKING AMERICAN: Well, I don't see how that's possible.

Silence. The Frenchman spoke up again, quietly. "Would you like your bed back?"

VINNIE K–LOOKING AMERICAN: Nah, man. I'm cool. I just wanted you to know that I know that you took that shit, man. Good night.

I memorized the sound of Vincent Kartheiser's voice and

thought: *Look out for this dude. He's willing to create a super-uncomfortable situation for no reason, and that is a dangerous trait.*

We woke up the next morning with a modest agenda. Go to the Van Gogh Museum, smoke tons of weed in a café, then go to a live sex show. It was all going swimmingly. Van Gogh was straight killing it, I smoked a little less weed than I did the previous day and didn't have a nervous breakdown, and we found ourselves in the part of our program where we were being led by a Nigerian man down a dark alley into a small, very empty, red-velvet theater, where people would have sex and we would watch them. We were pretty psyched.

Unfortunately, the show started slow. Very slow. So slow that after about twenty minutes of watching strippers of all genders—none of whom seemed nearly as thrilled to be there as we were—do their little dance routines, I started pushing to go out to the street to smoke a joint and then head back in by the time the sexing was going down. Ben wasn't that thrilled with the plan, not wanting to miss the sex part of the sex show.

I was like, "Don't worry, man. It'll be so fast."

He reluctantly caved. "We better not miss this shit."

As we were heading back through the narrow hallway after finishing our joint, I saw two VERY sweaty, VERY out-of-breath people walking away from the stage toward a small dressing room. Ben looked outraged.

BEN: **Shit! Those were the fuckers! The sex people! We missed them!**

ME: **Maybe not!**

BEN: **We totally fucking did! That was a post-sex look those people had! They were all sweaty and gross-looking. We for sure missed it.**

We got back to the theater, and sure enough, someone was wiping up the floor with a towel, the deed having been done. Ben was pissed, and I felt terrible. I ruined the live-sex-show experience, and it was a fucking bummer. We turned to go, but before we reached the door, the lights dimmed, and an announcer came on the speaker and said in a Dutch accent: "Alright, now all we have left is . . . the GRAND FI-NALE!"

We stopped. There was more. Thank god. A shot at redemption. Maybe this would be good enough that Ben wouldn't hate me forever. Maybe it would be even BETTER than the sex part of the show. I didn't know what that could possibly be, but, hey, "Grand Finale" were their words, not mine. We took our seats and a lovely woman took the stage. She then said something . . . startling.

"May I have a volunteer?"

Hmm. What could that mean? We'd seen a wide array of skill displayed here, so it was a question with a lot of implications. Not that there were a ton of people in the place, but nobody was taking the bait. The woman repeated the request.

"I said, may I have a volunteer?"

Before I even looked at Ben, I could feel his eyes boring through the side of my skull. I turned to him slowly. He was indeed staring back.

BEN: Volunteer.

ME: Oh, man, I don't want to.

BEN: You have to.

ME: I really don't want to.

BEN: I don't care, you have to! What are you afraid of?

ME: I don't wanna have sex in front of all these people. Or have her buttfuck me with a dildo or something. Nothing against that, like, as an act, it's just not something I wanna try for the first time in front of an audience.

BEN: I don't wanna see you have sex in front of all these people, but still, you gotta do it, man. We missed the sex part of the sex show because of you! We need to come out of this with something. Also, you're a performer! Imagine how that woman must feel right now! She's up there, naked, just wanting to do her grand fucking finale, and nobody will volunteer to do it! Get the fuck up there! Close the fucking show, man!!!

I couldn't deny his logic. I had to do it. It was the only way to make things right. I slowly raised my hand, hoping she wouldn't see it. She instantly did and was *thrilled* to have a taker and invited me onstage. I went up to what I could only describe as a nervous smattering of applause.

"Please take off your shirt."

Okay. Not a great start, but who knows, maybe we were going to wrestle or something. I took off my shirt and, to my dismay, was met with waves of laughter from the crowd. Uproarious laughter. Clapping. Knee-slapping. I mean, I'm no Timothée Chalamet, but I didn't think my body was worth laughing at hysterically. I looked down at myself, and there it was.

The fucking money belt.

It was protruding above my waistband for all to see and, more specifically, laugh super-duper hard at. Not only was it humiliating, it was a MASSIVE security breach. Now everyone in this place knew exactly where to look if they were gonna try to rob me.

So, there I am, onstage, money belt situated maybe three-quarters of the way to my belly button. What next?

"Please, lay on the floor, faceup."

Oy vey. Now, I'm no germaphobe, and I did not see *specifically* what happened on this stage, but I could imagine the culmination wasn't the type of thing that one would want to lie down in. Sure, I saw the tail end of a cleanup, but they weren't really putting much elbow grease into it. It was uninspired, like a waiter in a diner quickly wiping down a table.

Also, not for nothing, but me lying down on my back was a position sex might happen in, playing into my first fear— the fear of fucking on a stage in front of strangers and one friend. I looked at Ben sitting in the audience. He gestured: *Get down there.* I did, and as my bare back pressed against the floor, it felt clammy and wooden, like a giant Popsicle stick that someone had been sucking.

The lovely woman then produced a Sharpie, took off the cap, and inserted the back end of it in her vagina. She then squatted over me and proceeded to write on my torso, the pen firmly gripped by her cervix (I think? I don't know all the vagina parts by name!). None of us could tell what she was writing, but we were all rapt with anticipation. She finished, stood me up, and we all got to see the prestige: In PERFECT cursive, it said triumphantly, "THE END!"

This shit blew that *My Left Foot* shit out of the water. Daniel Day-Lewis can suck this lady's fucking dick. That dude might be the best actor on earth, but he ain't writing shit out on people's bodies with his vagina. I know what you're thinking—Daniel Day-Lewis doesn't have a vagina. Fine. Even if we gave him a pass and let him put the Sharpie in his bumhole, it would never have this level of penmanship. It was true art, and I was honored to be a part of it. It was one of the best rounds of applause I've ever heard, and, most important, Ben seemed happy.

We returned to the hostel, once again before any of our

roommates, and went to sleep. We needed to get to bed earlier than usual. We had a big day ahead of us. We were gonna do shrooms.

✿ ✿ ✿

The day's plan was deceptively simple:

1. Go buy shrooms.

2. Eat the shrooms.

3. Go to the grocery store and buy stuff for a picnic.

4. Go to the park and have a picnic as the shrooms kick in.

5. Hang out in the park and have a great time.

6. Go back to the youth hostel and go to sleep.

Things instantly went south. We got to the Smartshop, which is one of these little shops throughout Amsterdam that are filled with humid fish tanks where they cultivate hallucinogenic fungus. Normally, shrooms are all dried out and chewy, and we'd eat around three and a half grams each, which would usually amount to like three or four little dehydrated mushrooms, which is a solid amount.

We ordered from the man behind the counter.

Me: We'd like seven grams of your most hallucinogenic mushrooms, please.

Shroom Salesman: Seven grams?

Me: Yeah.

Shroom Salesman: We don't have seven grams.

BEN: Huh? How much do you have?

SHROOM SALESMAN: They come in packs of thirty grams, approximately.

ME: How many shrooms is that? Two hundred?

SHROOM SALESMAN: No, just one. Per pack.

He motioned toward these little Rubik's Cube–sized packages that each contained one fresh, wet mushroom.

Curveball. Hmm . . .

BEN: How many do most people eat?

SHROOM SALESMAN: It depends.

Me and Ben huddled.

ME: I mean, it's probably mostly water weight, right?

BEN: Yeah. A shroom is a shroom. The fact that it's dehydrated shouldn't make a difference. If anything, it's probably more concentrated because it's dehydrated.

ME: Yeah. We should just gauge it by the amount of mushrooms we'd normally eat, not the weight.

BEN: Yeah. Good call.

ME: So, we'd normally have like three big mushrooms each.

We turned back to the man behind the counter.

ME: We'll take ninety grams each please.

The guy looked at us a bit strangely, but in retrospect not NEARLY as strangely as he should have. He gave us the shrooms and we went outside, where we shoveled them into our faces.

Although inelegant, the first two steps were complete. Time for the next item on the agenda: Go to the grocery store and buy stuff for a picnic. Should be simple enough.

Now again, for those of you who aren't familiar with shrooms, they normally take between thirty and forty-five minutes to kick in, which should have been ample time to get what we needed and get to the park. But these were not normal mushrooms. And we had not taken a normal amount of them.

We were barely three steps into the store when Ben looked at me. "Holy shit."

If he was referring to the fact that every aisle in sight was undulating rhythmically and had a shimmer as though the sunlight (which was not present in the store) was being diffused by a giant whirling fan, each blade made of a different-color piece of glass (which was also not present in the store), then I knew what he meant. "Yeah, man. Holy shit is right."

"This shit is kicking in HARD."

I waved my hand in front of my face. It left trails of a thousand streaking lines. "Yeah, dude. Super fucking hard."

BEN: **Let's just get some shit and get the fuck out of here. This place is freaking me out.**

I tried to calm Ben down. "Yeah, man, no worries. Let's do this."

If you've ever been grocery shopping while an inhuman amount of hallucinogenic mushrooms are aggressively taking over your system, you know that shit ain't easy. I get overwhelmed grocery shopping when I'm completely sober. This was like trying to solve an algebra problem while trying to find my way out of a maze, while dealing with the fact that someone had apparently taken my brain out of my skull, strapped it to a rocket ship, and blasted it out into the farthest reaches of the cosmos. Suffice to say, it was a challenge.

Ben was getting . . . uncomfortable. "Let's just get some shit and GO!"

"Okay! Just chill!" I started putting stuff in the cart. It

didn't matter what. There was no way we'd be eating it. The cashier looked at me, eyes and mouth swirling around her face like a Picasso.

"I'll pay cash."

I gave her all the cash I had on me, which I really hoped was enough, and we hightailed it out of there. As we made our way toward the park, Ben had an intense, focused energy. "Let's just get through this" was the overall vibe he was giving off. I was tripping hard but didn't feel that bad—mentally. Physically, my stomach was turning on me. We hadn't eaten anything before downing the shrooms, and they are, for all intents and purposes, poisonous, so I was getting a nasty case of rotgut.

We made it to the park and dropped the shopping bag. Ben seemed relieved; I was dreading breaking the news.

ME: Yo, man.

BEN: Yeah?

ME: Uh . . . I think I gotta go find a bathroom.

BEN: NO!

ME: I have to.

BEN: I don't care!

ME: Why does it matter?

BEN: Because I don't want you to leave me alone here!

ME: So, come with me!

BEN: Fuck no! I can't walk anymore! I'm not doing well, man!

The sky was bright purple, so I knew where he was coming from.

ME: Look, dude, just wait here, chill, and I'll be back in, like, ten minutes. I'll find a coffee shop or restaurant or something and then I'll be right back.

Ben looked like a child who was being abandoned. "Fuck. Fine. Just be fast."

I tried my best to be fast. I really did. I speed-walked over to the main road, which made me start to sweat and made my heart beat faster, which made the drugs pump through my system more intensely, which in turn made my heart beat faster and made me sweat more, creating a bit of a cycle. I was running out of time. I saw a quaint little tea shop and burst through the front door. I have a clear recollection of the horrified looks on the faces of the Dutch employees.

"Can I use please use your restroom?!" I blurted out.

If those words were any indicator of my ability to control things coming out of me, I was in for a rough few minutes. They responded in Dutch in far too many words to mean "yes," but I took it as an affirmation, because the alternative would have been worse for everyone.

I barreled into a TINY little restroom and sat down as I proceeded to hallucinate intensely for an amount of time that, to this day, I couldn't even begin to estimate. Somewhere between ten minutes and nineteen thousand years. I assume I did all the things a person does to consider the experience successful and then sped out of the restaurant as fast as I could, not wanting to see the melting faces of the horrified staff. I made it out to the street, which was rolling like a choppy river.

Won't be crossing that, I thought. I headed back toward the park on a road that was crammed with foot traffic. I was actually feeling quite good. I had done it. Mission accomplished. All good in the hoo—

BLARGHHUUWWAAA!

I projectile-vomited on the sidewalk with such velocity that it splattered on the legs of a lot of nearby pedestrians. They looked at me with disgust, as the purple sky turned lime green and began flashing like a strobe light.

So close, I thought. *I just gotta make it back to Ben and we can have our picnic and everything will be fine.*

As soon as I rounded the corner into the park, I knew everything was not going to be fine. There was Ben, right where I left him, except now he was lying motionless, facedown in the grass, his arms firmly pressed to his sides. I ran over to him.

"Ben!"

He turned and looked at me. "Holy fuck! We gotta go!"

"Where?"

"I don't know! I just gotta get out of here!"

"Okay, let's go back to the hostel. We'll pack up the food we bought and—"

"No! Fuck it! Let's bail!"

Ben started quickly walking away from our nonsensical picnic. I followed, looking back, seeing our random ingredients shrink in the distance. A mess in an otherwise pristine park.

ME: What were you doing facedown?

BEN: I was hiding.

ME: From who?

BEN: Everyone was looking at me.

ME: I didn't see anyone looking at you.

BEN: That's because I was hiding.

The logic added up.

BEN: That was the worst moment of my life.

ME: Whoa, really?

BEN: Yeah. The worst moment.

ME: So right now we're like four minutes after the worst moment of your life?

BEN: Yep.

ME: That's heavy shit.
BEN: Sure is. Now I can't talk anymore.

And he didn't. We made it back to the hostel, Ben in silence the whole time. We got to the room and he got in bed and hid under the blanket. I was still tripping VERY hard and didn't just *want* to talk, I needed to. Then one of our roommates came into the room. He smiled.

"What's up, guys?"

As soon as he spoke, I recognized the voice; it was the bed guy from the first night in the hostel! The Vincent Kartheiser guy! The whirling tornado of awkwardness who sucked up all in his path.

"Not much," I said. "We're tripping pretty hard, and my buddy here is kinda out of commission for the time being."

"I hear that," he said. "Wanna smoke a joint?"

I wound up talking to annoying bed guy for a solid two hours, as Ben reassembled his consciousness to the point that he could communicate again. The guy turned out to be great. He was a skateboarder who was traveling around Europe alone. He'd been fucked with at a few hostels, so he was sensitive to the guy stealing his bed, and he seemed to feel bad about the whole incident. All in all, he was a fantastic dude.

After he left, Ben rejoined reality and put his hand on my shoulder. "We should leave this place."

ME: The hostel?
BEN: No. Amsterdam. Let's get on a train and go to Paris.

We weren't supposed to go for a few days, and I wasn't really sure where we would stay or how any of that would work, but nonetheless I nodded. "I'm fucking IN."

My agreeable nature likely had something to do with the

fact that, at this point, I was still FULLY on mushrooms. It had maybe been three hours since we took them; every shadow danced, and mouths didn't move according to the words coming out of them. We shoved our belongings in our giant backpacks and walked to the station, where we boarded our train to Paris.

We continued to trip the whole way, arriving in Paris in the middle of the night, wandering the streets as the haze of the shrooms lifted. We turned to each other.

BEN: **Where are we gonna stay?**

ME: **I have no idea.**

BEN: **Where are we? What neighborhood is this?**

ME: **I have no idea.**

Ben looked around.

BEN: **Why the fuck did we come to Paris?**

ME: **Honestly . . . I have no idea.**

We spotted the Eiffel Tower in the distance and arrived as the sun rose, and that's when it really hit us. We did so many shrooms we didn't just freak out, or throw up on the street, or litter a whole picnic's worth of food in one of the most beautiful parks in Holland. We did so many shrooms we wound up in a completely different country. So, if you're ever in Amsterdam and you're debating how many shrooms to buy from the Smartshop, err on the side of caution. And make sure your passport is securely hidden in your money belt, because you might need it.

DRINKING IN L.A.

After being on two failed TV shows, in 2001 I found myself in the same boat as a million other motherfuckers in L.A.—an unemployed actor/writer with a real chip on his shoulder that other people's shit was getting made and other people were getting parts he wasn't, which is a great look.

I was also pretty lonely and found it really hard to meet women that I got along with. I was the age of a college student, but I was in the adult work world, and I was gross. Not sexually gross, just young-dude gross. My apartment was disgusting. I think I didn't change my sheets for maybe six months? It literally didn't occur to me. It seemed like changing your rug, as in something you just don't do. There was no differentiation for me between the sheets and the mattress, and you don't change your mattress, right? At one point I just bought new sheets and put them over my old dirty ones.

Once, my apartment had a terrible fly infestation. My kitchen was SWARMED by hundreds and hundreds of flies, and for the life of me I couldn't figure out the cause. Someone told me that it might be a gas leak, as that can attract flies, which scared the shit out of me because I smoked all day every day, and the thought of poisoning myself or exploding myself wasn't awesome. I called the gas company to come check out the apartment.

The guy came with a little gas-detecting device, but no alerts sounded. "It's so weird. I just can't figure out what it is."

Then he walked over and opened a drawer under the sink. "Maybe it's this . . . ?"

There was an eggplant with a thick cloud of flies around it that must have been placed there about three months earlier and had melted into goop. So if you've ever wondered what happens to an eggplant that you leave in a drawer for three months, it melts and attracts flies and makes you realize you should probably make some better life choices. What the fuck was I doing buying an eggplant in the first place? I wasn't gonna cook that shit. Anyway . . .

I used to meet people when I went out and did stand-up comedy, but I had recently quit, because I wasn't that good at it. It was actually quite a bummer, but I'm glad I quit. I'd go out to clubs and see Sarah Silverman, David Cross, Zach Galifianakis, Bob Odenkirk, Paul F. Tompkins, just DESTROYING, and then I'd get up and not destroy. I was the worst thing you could be, which was just fine—good enough to keep going, but not great enough to really make an impression. I bailed, and over the years I watched a lot of them become super-famous, which made me feel even better about the choice. Sometimes quitting is great, I guess, which is not something they teach you as a kid. "Never quit, but sometimes do quit, 'cause you simply might not be that good at some shit."

It was around this time that L.A.'s nightlife was having a resurgence in the form of a few nightclubs that had I guess what you'd call "hot" nights. My friend Dave was friends with another guy who was a promoter for all these clubs, so we'd go out and basically try to meet women. It was a crazy scene. People dressed wild.

I remember being in a VIP room, drinking and hanging out with Rick James for an evening. He wore a sequined blazer and platform shoes, towering over everyone else in the club.

I remember being at a house party at Simon Cowell's, and there was a woman wearing what can only be described as a series of handkerchiefs sewn together into a dress.

ME: Who is that?

DAVE: I actually went to high school with her. Her dad owns the Hilton hotels! Her name is Paris.

I swear once I saw Owen Wilson at a club in a mink coat, so if that doesn't encapsulate the time, I don't know what does.

I think I went on a date with only one woman I met at a club, and it ended bizarrely. Alex was a friend of a friend. I called her a few days after we met, which seems barbaric today, and asked her out to dinner. We went and seemed to really hit it off. At the end of the night, we made out by her car and talked about seeing each other soon. I was totally smitten.

I called her the next day, because I have no game, and she didn't call me back. A few days went by, so I called again and left a message. A few days after that, she called and explained that she had gotten an audition for Lois Lane in the new Superman reboot starring Brandon Routh, directed by now-disgraced creepo Bryan Singer. She was learning her lines all week, which I totally understood. She said she'd call me after the audition, which she never did. I probably acted like an idiot in some way, so who can blame her. It just made me mad at myself for fucking things up.

But a couple weeks after our first date, I got some great news: I had an audition for a movie, which was always nerve-racking but the sign of a real opportunity. And it wasn't just any movie; it was the movie that was being made for the second season of *Project Greenlight,* a show I was fucking obsessed with.

In general, I love reality television, and *Project Greenlight* was one of the shows that made me a convert. If you don't know, *Project Greenlight* was a show created by Ben Affleck and Matt Damon, which posed the questions: "Does the Hollywood system work? Does it actually award the best filmmakers the opportunity to make films, or are there those out there who are just as talented but don't have the connections or opportunities?"

If you watched the show, the answer would seem to be "Yep! The Hollywood system works like a motherfucker," because all the movies to come out of *Project Greenlight* fucking suck butt. They also literally only picked white dudes to direct the movies in every single season of the show, so they weren't really granting opportunities to people who wouldn't have probably gotten them anyway.

But at the time, none of this was clear to me. It was just an exciting opportunity that was taking my mind off what an unlovable loser I was in my personal life.

The movie was called *The Battle of Shaker Heights,* and I
was auditioning for the funny friend of the main guy, which
was standard for me. I pulled up outside the office building
where the auditions were being held, walked into the waiting room, and saw two very shocking things:

The first was a giant camera in my face, filming me the
second I opened the door. I hadn't thought of it, but I realized in that moment that by auditioning to be in the *Project
Greenlight* movie, I was, by default, going to be on *Project
Greenlight,* because the process itself is the actual product.

The next thing I saw was that the only other actor waiting
in the small room was Alex, the girl who I had gone on the
date with a couple weeks earlier who didn't call me back.

My eyes WIDENED and the camera seemed to PUSH IN
on me dramatically.

Me: Hi.

The camera WHIP-PANNED over to Alex, who looked
from me to the camera and back to me.

Alex: Hi.

The camera WHIPPED back to me and followed me as I
slowly walked over to the only other chair, which was right
next to Alex. I sat down and the camera just locked in on us,
a tight TWO-SHOT.

Me: Hey.

Alex: Hey.

The camera operator seemed to sense the discomfort and
MOVED CLOSER, panning from one of us to the other.

All of a sudden, in real time, I found myself on a reality
show, running into a girl who didn't call me back after a date,
which was bittersweet because that would be the EXACT
type of shit that I'd wanna watch more than anything. We sat

in silence as the camera panned back and forth between us, the tension finally breaking when she was called into the room to read.

As a side note, auditioning is the fucking worst. A lot of the time, the room where the auditions are happening is right off the waiting room, and while you're sitting there, you can hear every other actor doing the scene before you, knowing all the while that they'll be able to hear you, too. You're often reading with a casting director or assistant, who is decidedly NOT an actor.

By far, the weirdest audition I ever did was for the movie *8 Mile*. The casting director, Mali Finn, decided that she didn't feel comfortable reading the off-camera dialogue, because of how . . . rapper-y it was? The role I was up for was a guy named Cheddar, and all his scenes were with Rabbit, who would be played by Eminem. Rather than find someone who she thought would be good to read with the actors, Mali told each actor that they were responsible for bringing someone to the audition to read with, which is fucking nuts.

I told Jason Segel about this, and he said he ALSO had an audition for Cheddar in *8 Mile*, and he ALSO was told to find someone to bring in to read opposite him. We asked our agents if our auditions could be scheduled one right after the other, so that one of us could audition for Cheddar, with the other reading the Rabbit part, and then we'd switch. We had a sleepover at my apartment the night before the auditions so we could rehearse and then carpooled to the audition together.

It wasn't until we were called into the room to read that we realized what a terrible idea it was. Auditioning is embarrassing in the best of times. Add the fact that one of my best friends is watching me do it and that we're both reading for rappers from Detroit, which we could NOT have been less right for.

I was gonna be Cheddar first, and Jason was Rabbit. We started.

JASON: Yo, yo, mothafucka! It's Chedda! What up, bitch!

And then I started laughing hysterically. And so did Jason. We literally couldn't make it through the auditions. As soon as one of us started the scene, the other would lose it.

ME: Yo, yo, Rabbit! You gotta record your shit at Paisley Park, yo!

JASON: Where, yo?

ME: Paisley Park, mothafucka!

It was so silly, we couldn't finish. We just excused ourselves and saw ourselves out, tears streaming down our faces.

♧ ♧ ♧

In 2004, I had been unemployed and single for about two years, and I was running out of all the money I had made on *Freaks and Geeks* and *Undeclared*. Judd Apatow VERY kindly let me help him on some of the movie rewrites he was doing, but me and Evan needed a real job. One day I got a call from Judd's manager, Jimmy Miller, who is Dennis Miller's brother and looks like what Dennis would look like if he was completely hairless.

JIMMY: Hey, Chachi!

(He doesn't talk like Dennis, but for the purposes of this anecdote, I'll make him.)

JIMMY: Look, hate to pull you out of your Mexican weed-induced stupor, but I have a client who needs writers like a sumo needs to pick his wedgie.

(Dennis Miller is not funny.)

ME: Who?

JIMMY: Alright, Chachi, it's for Sacha Baron Cohen. He's doing the second season of *Da Ali G Show* for HBO and he keeps firing all his writers, so we're looking for replacements. Go meet Sacha, pitch some ideas, see if he likes you.

I was speechless. I was completely obsessed with Sacha and *Ali G,* and had been since it was on British TV. I couldn't conceive of how I would contribute to a show that I idolized so much, so my first instinct was to say no.

ME: I'm not sure I can do that. . . . It's just . . . such a high level of work. I don't think he'll like us.

JIMMY: Okay, Chachi! Lemme know if you think of anyone who might be good.

I called Evan, who was still at university in Montreal, and told him. He lost it.

EVAN: You fucking said no?!

ME: Yeah. I mean, I don't even know how to write a show like that. He won't hire us.

EVAN: Who fucking cares?! We need to work, asshole! We should at least try, for fuck's sake! Call Jimmy back and tell him we want to meet! I'll fly in! Just call him the fuck back!

I did, and we had a meeting the next week. We knew Spring Break was coming up, and we pitched Bruno going to Spring Break to mess with frat guys. Sacha didn't even know what Spring Break was.

SACHA: How do you go to Spring Break? It's a time, not a place.

ME: No, we go to Florida, which is where everyone goes for Spring Break. Daytona Beach, Miami . . . that's where Spring Break IS!

Sometimes you pitch an idea so good that you get hired

just because the person you pitched knows it's an idea they need to use, and they'd feel guilty using it if they didn't hire you. They VERY often just steal it, so it shows Sacha's a good guy, because he hired us, which was super-exciting, because although we had completed the scripts for *Superbad* and *Pineapple Express,* they wouldn't be made for years, and this was my first official job working with Evan.

We wrote in what's known as the CNN Building on Sunset Boulevard in Hollywood, with a few other writers, all of whom were British and had worked on the original show. The only other non-Brit was a guy who was also our age, which was rare to see. His name was Will Reiser and he was a producer on the show—it was his job to book the guests that Sacha would interview in character. We quickly became good friends.

Soon after we started working there, a prevalent topic of conversation was that Will looked like shit. Not that he dressed like shit or anything. He just looked . . . sick. All the time. Weak, yellow; he had terrible skin. Also, his back hurt him all the time, which is unusual for a 120-pound dude in his early twenties. We thought maybe the stress of lying to people all day in order to secure the interviews was getting to him, but we were very wrong.

It turned out Will had a giant cancerous tumor wrapped around his spine. One of the biggest ones his doctors had ever seen. The next few months were crazy for him, and as one of his closest friends, a bit crazy for me, too, but with much lower stakes. They operated and successfully removed the tumor, and that started him on a very long recovery with dozens and dozens of follow-up appointments to monitor his progress.

At the time, Will was dating an actor, Amy, who had a

friend, Lauren, who she thought I would like. Some people we knew were having a birthday party at El Cid, a Mexican bar and restaurant in Silver Lake, and what I'll call a "soft setup" was happening.

I went to Amy's place to meet everyone and we were going to drive to El Cid together. I walked into the dining room and there was Lauren Miller. The second I saw her I thought, *Oh no . . . I could spend the rest of my life with this person.* She was funny, smart, beautiful, and she had programmed her cellphone ring to be the theme from *Jurassic Park,* and if that doesn't make you fall for someone, I don't know what does.

But I don't think Lauren felt the same because she was mostly talking about the fact that the night before, she had been on a date with a guy she liked, and she heard that he was also going to be at the party and was psyched to see him. Again, I don't have any "game" as it were, but I wanted to seem attractive, so I thought, *What better approach than to be the super-nice, creative, funny friend of the guy who has cancer.* And, thankfully, Will was more than happy to help me play that role, so it all kinda worked.

The big topic of conversation for the night became me trying to convince Will to write about his cancer experience and turn it into a movie.

ME: A cancer comedy! Who doesn't want that?

WILL: You can play my friend who's supportive but also kind of using my situation for his own personal gain, which is a HUGE stretch, but I think you can do it.

We all went to a diner and joked around about Will's cancer till 2 A.M.

Two great things came from the night: Will did write the movie, and I produced it and acted in it, and it became *50/50,* which is definitely one of the best things we've ever made.

Also, Lauren seemed to stop talking about the other guy and shifted her focus to me instead.

Will called me the next day and told me that Lauren liked me, so I phoned her and asked her out. I asked her if she wanted to play mini golf, which is a good couple of hours of straight talking, which is a risk, but I bet on myself conversationally.

We liked each other, and after the round I asked her if she wanted to go to the 101 Coffee Shop and get a brownie waffle sundae, to which she was like, "Fuck yeah!" which only made me like her more.

We were driving along the busy 101 freeway on the way to dessert, and the whole time I was thinking, *How do I make contact? A shoulder touch? Touch her hand? Maybe while we're eating the sundae, we'll share a spoon? That'll be intimate. A good step in the right direction. Should I have shaken her hand after the golf round? That would have been smooth. First contact is always tough.* Then—BOOOOOOM!!!

A car doing around seventy miles an hour SLAMMED into the back corner of my car, which was doing about sixty. We spun out and slid across all four lanes of the highway. I remember seeing the headlights of cars coming at us as we rotated, which isn't something you wanna see on the freeway. We SMASHED into the wall along the shoulder with a CRASH. The car that hit us didn't even slow down; it just ripped off down the road.

I turned to Lauren. "Are you okay?!"

"Yes. Are you okay?"

"Yeah . . . I think so . . ."

"Holy shit."

We sat there for a moment to process what happened. We were, miraculously, both fine. My car was totaled, and they had to shut down the freeway for a minute to tow it off the road and on to Coldwater Canyon, which coincidentally was right near where Lauren lived. Her roommate was nice enough to pick us up and drive me home.

I got out of the car in front of my apartment, and Lauren did, too. We hugged. Contact.

I kept calling and asking her out, and she kept saying yes. Our second date was to go see the new movie *Cinderella Man*, starring Russell Crowe. I was so nervous. I remember I had a small pimple on the side of my forehead that I just couldn't stop picking at. It was terrible. I was standing in front of the mirror, yelling, "Stop! Stop trying to pop this thing, you idiot! It's not ready!!" But my hands wouldn't listen. They kept squeezing.

I ended up with a massive contusion on my head that I covered with a Band-Aid, and although I hate lying, I told her that I was play-fighting with a friend and scraped my face, which, although stupid, sounded better than "I was really nervous about kissing you, so I ripped a giant fucking chunk out of my head while screaming at myself."

That night we kissed for the first time.

I knew I was in love with her a few months later. My friend Nick was having his bachelor party in Cabo San Lucas, Mexico. He rented a big house, and a bunch of young men stayed there together, with a chef cooking food for us all. I kept being warned about drinking the water and eating rinsed produce, but I was like, "Fuck it, what's a Mexican bachelor party without freshly washed lettuce." So I indulged.

I was on the same flight back as another dude from the party, and when we were landing, he asked how I was getting home.

"My girlfriend is picking me up!"

He looked at me longingly.

"That's what I want . . ." he said.

That night, she slept over at my place, and I got up early the next morning to walk her out to her car, which I had gotten in the habit of doing. I pulled on my pants and checked myself out in the mirror. I remember thinking, *Look at you. You're in a meaningful relationship with a wonderful woman. She's picking you up from the airport. You're walking her to her car. There's mutual respect and care . . . you're really doing it.*

And then I thought I was farting, but I shat my pants, terribly.

There was no question that I shat my pants, and I only point that out because sometimes there IS a question as to whether or not you shat your pants. You ask yourself: "Was that a wet fart? Or was there more?" And then you check to make sure all is as it should be.

I didn't have to check; I knew nothing was as it should be. It was full on.

Lauren poked her head into the room. "Ready!"

Images of excessively rinsed Mexican carrots flooded my head. Poop flooded my pants.

I lived on the second story of a fourplex, so in order to get to Lauren's car, I'd have to go out of my bathroom, down the hall, down a flight of stairs, and then, depending on where she'd parked, a few dozen feet to her car.

"Alright! Let's go!"

I tried to look normal and confident, not like a guy who just pooped himself, as I took her hand and walked her down the stairs. Each step was a waking nightmare. I prayed to whatever god there is that she didn't smell anything, or that I didn't, either, because I worried that I would throw up if I did, which obviously wouldn't help things.

We made it outside, and I saw that she was parked about half a block up. I swung her hand as we walked, thinking, *How am I gonna kiss her goodbye while making sure my ass stays as far away from her nose as humanly possible?* I pulled off a kinda butt-out hug type thing.

I stood on the street and watched her pull away in her little Acura Integra, a Dave Matthews Band fire-dancer sticker on the back windshield, because as a young Jewish woman, she's legally obligated to have that. I thought to myself, *I'm gonna have to throw these underpants, pants, and at this point maybe my shoes and socks in the garbage.*

I also thought, *I love her, and I hope I get to spend the rest of my life with her and that one day I can tell her about this, because if anyone would appreciate this story, it's her.*

2012

wo things to know going into this:

First, Art Bell's *Coast to Coast AM* was a radio show that started in 1988, and by 1998 it was one of the most-listened-to late-night radio shows in the world. Art took calls from people looking to talk about aliens, werewolves, the occult, Area 51, MK Ultra, and shit like that. He even had a regular caller who claimed to be a time traveler, and he would warn listeners of future catastrophes.

As a new resident to Los Angeles, I found myself driving around a lot late at night, and I loved listening to Art Bell and the severely open-minded weirdos who would call in to the show. Of all the crazy shit people would talk about, one of the most prevalent topics, heralded by the weirdest of the weirdos, was that the world was going to end in 2012. There were a bunch of random things that pointed to this outcome, the most "convincing" being that the Mayan calendar ended on December 21, 2012. I don't know much about the Mayans other than they're the bad guys in *Apocalypto,* the Mel Gibson movie that I'd recommend if he wasn't a drunken anti-Semite. Either way, from 1998 onward I had been conditioned to think one thing above all else: If you thought the world was going to end in 2012, you were a bit of an odd duck.

Second, *The Last Starfighter* is a great movie from 1984, about a kid who's a loser in his real life but he's amazing at playing videogames. He then learns that his videogame skills actually allow him to save the world. Evan and I had tried to get the rights to the movie for a sequel or remake from the time we got to Los Angeles, but the original screenwriter, Jonathan R. Betuel, owns the rights and refuses to let anyone touch the property—and I don't blame him, because it's perfect.

In early 2012, Evan and I got an exciting call: Steven Spielberg wanted to meet with us. This was, for all intents and purposes, pretty fucking dope. I had met him a couple times very briefly at some parties in the past. He's a nice enough guy, and I think I'd be MUCH more intimidated by him if he didn't remind me so much of my father-in-law, who is a lovely, unintimidating man.

Steven Spielberg   My father-in-law

Similarities to my father-in-law aside, we were excited. We pulled into the DreamWorks part of the Universal lot, which has a giant *Jurassic Park*–style gate that opens slowly. We played the theme song on my phone as we entered.

We were greeted in the lobby by a receptionist flanked by a film camera from the 1940s and a model of a Tyrannosaurus rex. After a few moments of quietly wondering if we'd smoked too much weed before this meeting (we had), we were brought up to Steven's office.

We walked past Norman Rockwell painting after Norman Rockwell painting (I think Spielberg has the largest private collection in the world) and were led into his office, where we were told to sit and wait, which we were more than happy to do.

What happened next shocks me to this day and, if you're a movie fan like I am, is really quite special and miraculous: Steven Spielberg came into the room *with* George Lucas. The two people responsible for most of the cultural touchstones of my childhood, together. *I'm meeting my HEROES!* I thought, not remembering the apt saying about just such an occasion.

The first thing that struck me was that George Lucas was wearing a denim shirt and jeans, which is a red flag. A lot of billionaire dudes seem to adopt this look, and I find it appalling. And perhaps the most painful insult toward my countrymen is that people call this a "Canadian tuxedo." We have real tuxedos in Canada, and they're lined with the finest narwhal blubber and lubricated in the most sugary of maple syrups.

Steven introduced us to George and rattled off some of our credits, none of which George had heard of.

I asked George what he'd been up to, and he took a seat

across from me and Evan, looked us dead in the eyes, and said, "Well, things have been pretty busy, considering we're nearing the end of 2012."

Hmmmmm . . . this sounded vaguely familiar to me. "What do you mean?"

"Well," he said, adjusting his denim shirt, "you know the world is going to end this year, right?"

I mean, I guess I shouldn't have been surprised. The notion that a dude who conceived of an entire science-fiction universe, complete with its own religion, mythology, technology, and hairstyles, would be a true weirdo seems obvious. But it was shocking, nonetheless.

"Uh . . . are you serious?" Evan asked.

"Very." George settled in. "What do you know about the San Andreas Fault?"

At this point, I noticed Spielberg at the desk behind George rolling his eyes, like, "Here we go again."

ME: What should we know about the San Andreas Fault?

GEORGE: That it's gonna fracture and everything west of it is gonna sink into the ocean, reshaping the world as we know it.

Me and Evan scanned his face, looking for any shred of irony, like Mandalorians scanning the cargo hold of the *Millennium Falcon* for stowaways (sorry). There was none.

EVAN: You really think that's gonna happen?

GEORGE: I know it's gonna happen.

ME: How?

GEORGE: It's science. And I know science.

Now, I don't doubt that once you're super-duper-duper rich, you get access to all sorts of shit that people who are *not* super-duper-duper rich don't get. Could it be that somewhere within that wealth of access to scientific facts was the knowledge of the inevitable fracturing of our continent? Who knows? If anyone knew, maybe it would be him.

Or maybe he meant "I know science *fiction*." Which he does, very well! And I get that if you know how to do a fake version of something well enough, you maybe start to think you can also do the real version of that thing. I remember being so good at the Rock Band videogame that I was almost convinced I could actually play drums on a Weezer song. But whether it's true or not, it was a fucking weird conversation to dive into. We just met this dude. It was essentially: "How's it going?" "Not bad, except the fucking world is gonna end soon, you stupid moron," which is, in my opinion, an awkward way to start a general meeting.

We tried to plow onward.

ME: Good thing Skywalker Ranch is east of the fault line!
GEORGE: It IS a good thing, and it's not a coincidence.

Oh, man.

Evan tried to make a joke. "Well . . . if you've got a spaceship hidden there somewhere, maybe save us a couple spots for after the Big One hits."

George then gave us a look that clearly articulated two things:

1. He *does* in fact have a fucking spaceship.

2. We *cannot* have seats on it.

Spielberg came over and tapped George on the shoulder. "Alright, we got a movie to talk about."

"I used to make those," George said. "Now I'm just a humble toymaker."

He left, and we all shared a look that very clearly said,

"Sure, he's strange, but he came up with lightsabers, so I guess we'll cut him some slack."

Then the Spielberg portion of the meeting commenced.

"I have an idea about a kid who's a loser in his real life but he's amazing at playing videogames, and then he learns that his videogame skills actually allow him to save the world."

Evan and I looked at each other.

ME: Uh . . . like *The Last Starfighter*?

STEVEN: You've heard of *The Last Starfighter*?

ME: Of course we have! We've been trying to get the rights to remake it, but the dude who owns the rights won't give them up!

STEVEN: I KNOW! It's so annoying! It'd be so good as a remake!

EVAN: We know!

STEVEN: Well, if you guys want to write a version of that idea, we'd love to make it at DreamWorks.

We left the meeting in a daze. I remember Evan saying in the car, "If we're gonna rip off *The Last Starfighter*, I'm not sure we need Steven Spielberg to do it with us. We can probably just rip that shit off by ourselves."

☆ ☆ ☆

Years later, we helped create the show *Future Man*, which is about a loser who's amazing at playing videogames and realizes his skills will allow him to save the world. That very same year, Spielberg released *Ready Player One*, about a loser who's amazing at playing videogames and realizes his skills will allow him to save the world.

I sometimes think about what an uncomfortable day December 12, 2012, must have been at Skywalker Ranch.

George and his friends all strapped into his spaceship, ready to feel the first tremors of the Big One as they hit the ignition button and launched into space. Was he happy when it didn't happen? Was he disappointed? Either way, my guess is he funneled all that paranoid skepticism into becoming a flat-earther.

They say never meet your heroes. I say meet them, just be ready for them to not invite you onto their spaceship.

ANGRY WHOPPER

I obviously tell a huge amount of drug-related stories throughout this book, and while most of them were events I look back on fondly, I feel like I should include a few exclusively cautionary tales about the devil's lettuce, ree-fers . . . MARIJUANA!!!

TALE 1

Flying sucks. Flying early in the morning on no sleep sucks even more. And flying early in the morning on no sleep while incredibly hungover is something that so obviously fucking sucks, if you find yourself doing it, you really only have yourself to blame.

A few years ago, I found myself doing this for the billionth time, wondering how I could be so stupid again. But this time . . . I had a plan. Someone had given me a weed brownie. A very strong weed brownie.

Some of the only times in my life where I truly thought, *Wow, I am TOO FUCKING HIGH,* have come after eating weed food. Once I ate a weed lollipop at the Golden Globes and got so high, I had to leave early. Weed brownies, in general, are wildly unpredictable. They range from being bad-tasting brownies that do nothing to heavy narcotics that make you feel like a character in *Trainspotting.*

I ate the brownie on the way to the airport, which would ultimately be the first of a few bad decisions.

I went through security as the brownie was starting to kick in. I then found myself hungover *and* incredibly high, and I was starting to panic a little. I had a three-hour flight to Vancouver ahead of me. I needed to come down and normalize in some way. I needed food.

The LAX terminals are a crazy crapshoot as far as what's available where. Some terminals have five-star French restaurants; others have people grilling dead rats over flaming garbage cans. And they have the nerve to charge twenty-four dollars for them, when dead rat is like thirteen dollars tops outside of the airport.

And then . . . I saw it. A place firmly nestled between nice eatery and dead-rat grillery: Burger King.

As far as fast food goes, I rank it like this: There's the better-than-normal fast-food chains, like Shake Shack and In-N-Out Burger, which are at the top. Chick-fil-A is delicious, but they're religious bigots, so we'll just put them in their own bucket. There's "fried chicken–based fast food," which Popeyes dominates, followed by Church's and KFC. Then there's the "normal" ones, which go:

1. McDonald's: You can't fuck with McDonald's. Once they added the McFlurry and became more

liberal with their breakfast hours, they were unstoppable.

2. Wendy's: The square burger is fucking great, their buffalo sauce is good with their nuggets, and a Frosty with French fries shoved inside it is arguably one of the greatest desserts on the planet.

3. Jack in the Box: Controversial third place, I know. Their late-night menu is fantastic. The "tacos," or whatever they are, are delicious. Between 2002 and 2005, I actually thought the Chicken Fajita Pita was healthy and ate about five of them a week. But it's their seasoned curly fries that earn them this spot.

4. Carl's Jr.: They have a burger with onion rings on it.

5. Burger King . . .

It was my only option, and I was resigned to having a Whopper, when something on the menu caught my eye: the Angry Whopper.

It was a Whopper with jalapeño peppers, pepper jack cheese, and spicy chipotle. My incredibly weakened brain thought, *Perfect.*

I ordered it, and even the guy behind the counter gave me a look like, "Really? You want *that*? *Now?!*" I gave him a nod, like, "Yeah . . . I do want that. I know it sounds crazy, but maybe I'm just crazy enough to get myself out of this hungover, weed-brownie stupor. And maybe this bizarre, insane burger that for some unexplainable reason is being offered up at 7:45 A.M. will knock my system back to normal." Like the grilled meat sandwich version of electroshock therapy.

I ate the Angry Whopper VERY FAST. I'm a very fast eater, to the point that Lauren is still amazed by it. She's eaten thousands of meals with me and is still like, "You take such big bites!" For something to be astounding for seventeen years, it must really be something. It actually tasted pretty good, because the spiciness carpet-bombed most of the natural Burger King flavors.

Right after I finished, I boarded the plane, and the Angry Whopper and weed brownie did what I'd hoped they'd do and knocked me unconscious before the plane even took off. I was hoping for an "asleep before takeoff, awakened by landing" situation, but that's rare. It's really the holy grail of sleep-flying. But that did not happen.

About two hours later, I was violently shaken awake by one of the flight attendants. I opened my eyes, scared and disoriented. The attendant yelled, "Sir! Be calm! You've just had a seizure!!!"

My first thought was *That's strange. I really don't feel like I had a seizure*—not that I'd ever had a seizure, so I didn't know what it felt like. But I actually felt way better than I did when I got on the plane. I was absolutely drenched in sweat, but that wasn't exactly a remarkable event for me. Still, I wasn't sure I *hadn't* had a seizure, and the flight attendant seemed VERY sure I had.

Then the flight attendant yelled, "Is there a doctor on the plane?!"

A hand shot up. "Yes! I'm a doctor!"

FLIGHT ATTENDANT: **This man has just had a seizure!**

DOCTOR: **Oh no!**

He ran over and pulled out one of those little flashlight pens that only doctors seem to have access to.

DOCTOR: **Are you sore? Do you feel okay?**

ME: Uh . . . I think I feel okay.

DOCTOR: This amount of sweat is not okay!

It was all happening so fast. I was following his finger as he was waving it around, and it occurred to me, *Maybe I didn't have a seizure. Maybe it was the Angry Whopper trying to escape my body through my pores.* I didn't want to name-drop the Angry Whopper specifically, and the doctor seemed to be wrapping up his checkup, so I thought I'd ride it out.

DOCTOR: Just keep drinking water until we land. Let me know if you feel off.

He left and I noticed a woman in a velour tracksuit beside me who had been silently watching the whole thing from her seat. I turned to her.

ME: Hi. I'm not sure you've seen what's been playing out over here, but . . . do you think I had a seizure?

VELOUR TRACKSUIT: I do not think you had a seizure.

ME: I don't, either.

VELOUR TRACKSUIT: I think you were just sleeping in a funny position, with your head kind of cocked back, and your mouth was open, and we were hitting a bit of turbulence, so your head started bouncing around in a weird way, and with all the sweating, I think the flight attendant was confused.

ME: Okay, me, too.

I sipped a bottle of water throughout landing, and as the plane started to make its way to the gate, the flight attendant came up to me.

FLIGHT ATTENDANT: Be calm. I'm going to tell everyone to stay in their seats. You can deplane and meet the paramedics who are waiting for you at the gate.

Oh god. I didn't want to cause a huge scene, so at this point, in my head, I'm like, *Okay, just go, talk to them, they'll see you're fine, they'll let you go, it'll be cool.*

I walked down the Jetway and saw a paramedic standing there with a wheelchair.

Paramedic: Hello, please sit down, sir.

Me: Look . . . I really—

Paramedic: Please sit down. You might be in shock. Let us check you out.

I reluctantly sat down in the wheelchair and started being pushed through the terminal. I'm thinking, *Okay, we'll just get to the street, and I'll explain to them—*

Another paramedic ran up. "Okay, I see you got him. The ambulance is waiting at the curb! We're ready for transport to the emergency room!"

This had gone too far. I had to fess up.

I stood. . . . They were shocked. It was like a scene in a movie where a paralyzed person is suddenly able to walk.

Me: This must stop! It has gone too far! I did not have a seizure! I am hungover, I ate a very strong weed brownie and an Angry Whopper!

I fled from the scene. I can only assume the paramedics were standing there, watching me go, thinking, *Yep, that makes sense.*

TALE 2

Lauren's father loves magic, so, not that long ago, we got tickets to see a magic show in Beverly Hills with her father, Scott, and his lady friend, Gaye, which is an old lady name if I've ever heard one. When we picked them up, Scott mentioned that he hadn't had anything to eat or drink all day, which isn't that uncommon for him. Like a lot of older guys, he takes a huge amount of pride in not taking good care of himself.

The magic show was at the Waldorf off of Wilshire. We got there a few minutes early and ordered drinks from the makeshift bar that was set up. The second after we got our drinks, they opened the doors to the theater and told everyone that seating was first come, first served, and that drinks weren't allowed. We wanted good seats, so we all chugged our drinks and sat down.

The show was great, but for me, the better the magic I'm watching, the more I'm distracted by what a weirdo this person must be to have spent that much time alone in front of a mirror to get that great.

After the show, we were all starving. We were in Beverly Hills, and Mastro's Steakhouse was nearby. Mastro's is kind of a bizarre mix of old-school steakhouse and nightclub. It's loud and packed, but they serve grilled meat, so it works out. They also have an amazing seafood tower. I love a seafood tower and think more food should be served in tower formation. Sometimes pizzas get a little platform, but they're really not living up to their potential.

As we were driving over there, Lauren started smoking a joint. Gaye asked for a hit, so we passed the joint back and she took a drag. We asked Scott, "You want a hit, too?"

He took a BIG hit and instantly started coughing his ass off. And kept coughing . . . and coughing. About five minutes into the eight-minute ride, he was still coughing. I turned to Lauren: "He's gonna be reeeeeeeal high."

We pulled into the valet and he was still coughing. We walked up to the host stand—still coughing. He was hacking up a lung. As we were being walked to our table, he was able to turn to me and wheeze out, "That was a big hit!"

We sat down, Lauren and Gaye taking the bench against

the wall facing the dining room, and Scott and me taking the two chairs opposite them. Scott finally stopped coughing, but now the weed was starting to hit him. He was looking around the restaurant like a newborn baby taking in a dazzling environment. (I will now switch to PRESENT TENSE because books about writing say it "adds immediacy to the story.")

SCOTT: **Wowww . . .**

LAUREN: **You okay, Dad?**

SCOTT: **Yep, fine.**

LAUREN: **You don't look fine.**

SCOTT: **I think I just need to use the restroom.**

Scott shoots up from the table and starts making his way through the restaurant. Then I see a look of terror sweep across Lauren's face. "Seth, go! Go get him! He's going down!"

I turn to see Scott in the middle of the dining room, wobbling. I leap up from my seat and run across the restaurant, hooking my arms under his armpits just as his legs completely give out from under him. His body goes limp and I struggle to hold him up. I see an empty chair beside me and plop him into it.

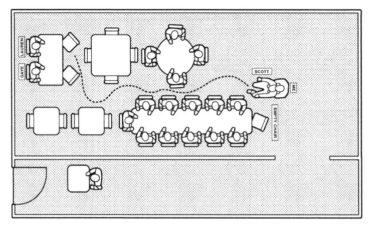

I can now see that he is basically unconscious, his body balanced in the chair shockingly well. He's propped up in kind of a *Weekend at Bernie's*–esque way. If he had sunglasses on, he would almost look normal.

I then look around and realize that this chair I put him in is actually at the head of a table of about twelve people. They are all staring at me and Scott, not really knowing what to say, and before I can explain anything, a fleet of servers appears and starts placing food in front of them, not noticing that there is a maybe-dead man at the head of the table.

SERVER: **Here's your steak! Here's your creamed spinach!**

He notices Scott.

SERVER: **What did he order? I don't think I have anything for him.**

ME: **Umm . . . nothing. He's just . . . uh . . . chilling here for a second.**

The manager, who must have seen it all go down, comes over.

MANAGER: **Is everything okay? Should I call an ambulance?**

ME: **No! No! It's fine. He . . . hasn't eaten very much today and he stood up too fast. I really think he's fine. Right, Scott?**

SCOTT: **Hrm . . . flurmmmm . . .**

ME: **Uh . . . see? He's fine. He just needs a minute.**

MANAGER: **Are you sure?**

I think, I'm *pretty* sure. But ultimately, I'm worried that making a big scene will make the situation worse. He isn't just passing out. He is passing out because he's way too high, which is a whole other category of passing out. You gotta tread lightly or a tailspin can occur. He doesn't need an escalation to this scene.

As someone who can smoke just about any amount of

weed and not have it affect them negatively, I'm always having to remind myself that it's something that can conceptually even happen. The idea of *smoking* an amount of weed that could incapacitate me seems impossible, so I've probably led a few people astray over the years. Still, at this moment, I don't think Scott needs to or wants to or should get an ambulance.

ME: I'm sure. He's fine. Just had too much wine, stood up too fast. Let's give him a minute. He'll be fine.

MANAGER: . . . Okay.

The manager leaves, and I turn back to Scott, who still looks like a corpse. I look at the table that he's presiding over, and they're all staring at me with their food in front of them.

ME: He's fine. Go ahead. Eat. It's fine.

They hesitantly start to eat their dinners, keeping one eye on me and Scott the whole time. I can hear them thinking, *Are we eating iceberg wedges with a rotting cadaver at our table?* But still, they keep eating.

A few moments later, Scott starts coming to.

ME: Are you okay?

SCOTT: Yeah, I'm fine. I just stood up too fast.

ME: Are you sure? Do you need an ambulance? Do you want to leave?

SCOTT: No. We came for dinner. Let's eat.

He gets up very slowly and I help him back to his seat. Everyone in the restaurant is looking on like, "Oh thank god, this fucking guy is alive."

We sit back down at our table.

LAUREN: Are you okay?!

SCOTT: Yeah. That hit of weed was so big, and the wine, and I just stood up too fast.

LAUREN: **Should we go?**

SCOTT: **No, I'm fine.**

The waiter appears at the table, doing his best to act perky.

WAITER: **Whoa! Everyone alright?!**

SCOTT: **Yep, fine!**

WAITER: **So . . . you'll *still* be joining us for dinner?**

SCOTT: **Yep. I'm fine. When I say I'm fine, I'm fine. We're not leaving on account of me.**

It's hard to argue with.

WAITER: **Alright! Here're some menus.**

When he hands them to us, Scott's head starts kind of bobbling around again. He does not look well. I can feel everyone in the restaurant looking at us like, "These lunatics are going to sit at this table while this man dies, because they want to eat a fucking porterhouse?!" Which isn't true but isn't 100 percent untrue, either.

SCOTT: **I'm hot.**

ME: **We'll order you some water when the waiter comes back.**

SCOTT: **I still have to go to the bathroom.**

LAUREN: **Maybe sit for a second and then you can go.**

SCOTT: **Okay . . . fine . . .**

My phone dings. It's a text from Lauren, messaging me from across the table.

LAUREN'S TEXT: **Should we go?**

MY TEXT: **He says he's okay. He's clearly just incredibly high. Honestly, food is probably the best thing for him.**

LAUREN'S TEXT: **I also just don't want to embarrass him.**

MY TEXT: **That ship has sailed.**

LAUREN'S TEXT: **Well, embarrass him MORE, I guess. He'll feel terrible if he feels like he ruined the night—**

Lauren's Voice: Oh no! Seth!

I look beside me, and Scott is trying to take off his belt and unbutton his pants.

Gaye: Scott! No!

Scott: I'm fine.

Me: Alright, let's go!

I buckle his belt and help him stand. Lauren and Gaye lead him toward the door, and I tip the waiter all the money I have on me.

Waiter: Is he okay? Is he having a stroke?

Me: No. He's incredibly stoned.

A huge smile comes across his face.

Waiter: Oh, thank fucking god! We've all been there, man!

By the time I get outside, Lauren and Gaye have lowered Scott onto a bench by the valet station. They're lifting a bottle of water to his lips like he's just been rescued from some desert island. We get him home, where he passes out on the toilet for the next three hours, a little prince on his throne. I don't know what it is about Scott's center of gravity, but the man can maintain a seated position while completely unconscious to a degree that I've never seen before or since. (I will now revert back to past tense. Thank you for going on this amazing literary journey with me.)

Lauren and I were driving to his house the next morning to say hi, and we were a little nervous. We really didn't want him to feel bad. And we especially didn't want the incident to deter him from going out and doing fun things, which, after a decade of being the caretaker for his dying wife, he was finally starting to do again. We were half-expecting a worst-case scenario of him saying, "I'm never going out again. This is what happens when you leave the house!"

We walked up to the door, and he opened it. A big smile on his face.

"I got too fucking high last night! Holy shit, that was crazy!"

He knew getting too high was nothing to be embarrassed by. It happens to the best of us.

FACE/OFF

Nicolas Cage is an odd, magnetizing, confusing man, whose bravery and talent are almost unmatched in his field. His performances as both Castor Troy *and* Sean Archer in the 1997 action extravaganza *FACE/OFF* are wild and wonderful, as he truly convinces the viewer that they've just witnessed an FBI agent switch faces with a crime lord in an attempt to go undercover in a prison where all the inmates wear magnetized boots in order to find the location of a hidden explosive device somewhere in Los Angeles. Also, I read that he owns a Tyrannosaurus skull, which is objectively bad-ass as hell. But as he stood across from me one fateful night in 2008, I thought, "Man, maybe we shouldn't have signed on to write *The Green Hornet*." But let me go back.

Me and Evan grew up loving comic books and action comedies, and we really thought we could contribute creatively to those spaces. We wrote a draft of a script for *The Green Hornet*, a radio show that was later turned into a comic book that was later turned into a TV series, which most famously starred Bruce Lee as Kato, the Hornet's much more formidable partner. The studio liked the draft enough that they told us we could start looking for directors.

There was really only one name we had in mind, and it was perfect because if it worked out, he could both direct the film and play Kato. We wanted Chinese actor/director Stephen Chow, who had recently made the film *Kung Fu Hustle,* which was fucking dope as fuck.

He read the draft and flew to L.A. to meet us. We really seemed to get along and he said he would love to work with us; he just had a few small notes on the script. We were thrilled.

He went back to Hong Kong, and a few weeks later we received an email from him that wasn't a few notes on our script but an outline for an entirely new version of the movie. We were thrown at first, but honestly, we really loved the guy's work, so we were excited to see what he had come up with, fully accepting that it was likely better than what we had come up with. I remember printing it out, and when I sat down to read it, something caught my eye. Near the bottom of the page, nestled in a paragraph I hadn't yet read, was the word "AIDS."

It really stood out because of the capitalization, much like it does on this page you're reading now.

I thought, *What's that word doing there? That's a weird thing to have in this outline for a comic-book action comedy. Oh well, I guess I'll just keep reading, and hopefully by the time I get there, it'll make sense. Maybe it's a metaphor? Or it stands for something else in Hong Kong? I'm sure it'll all make sense!*

Well, it did NOT make sense. What it turned out to be was a joke wherein the Hornet finds out that Kato had slept with his girlfriend, so he tells Kato that he has AIDS, hoping to fool Kato into thinking he would then also have AIDS. Needless to say, this was fucking batshit crazy, especially for a PG-13 superhero movie.

It seemed like our sensibilities were not exactly jiving, so we agreed to part ways with him as director, but he would still play Kato.

After a long process, we replaced him with French music-video and film director Michel Gondry, a hilarious and eccentric little man, which is a description that I know will enrage him, and then make him laugh.

Over the next few months, me, Evan, and Gondry would work on the script and send drafts to Chow, who kept refusing to sign his contract and fully commit to the movie. We got into a process that I'm sure was frustrating for everyone, where we would send him the script, he would send notes, we would try our best to do them, likely not do them that well, send the script back, and then he'd send more notes. It culminated in him wanting to come back from Hong Kong to meet one more time to give us notes. We were very willing to hear them, but only if Chow would commit to the movie before he came. I'm not sure it was a completely reasonable request: "You know how we've never been able to do what you've asked, well just sign on in the hope of that one day, despite there being NO evidence that it's possible . . . we will!" It was starting to feel like a real potential waste of time to keep rewriting the movie for an actor who might not even be in it ultimately. I think Gondry's exact words were "Tell him not to get on the plane if he isn't one hundred percent committed to being in the movie."

He showed up and his first words were "Before I commit to this, there are a few things we need to fix in the script."

And Gondry fucking lost it.

MICHEL (IN AN INCREDIBLY THICK FRENCH ACCENT): You 'ave no re-spect! You jerk us around like fools! Thees eez OVER!!

STEPHEN (COOL): Alright. I understand. It's unfortunate you feel that way. Let's just shake hands and end this on a good note.

MICHEL: NOOO! I WEEL NOT!!

It was cold as fuck, but at the time I respected it.

Now we had no Kato, and the studio very much pushed us to hire Taiwanese pop star Jay Chou, who was awesome although he literally spoke no English whatsoever, which is not ideal for a buddy comedy. They still had no faith in the film, so it became this paint-by-numbers casting game. Basically, if we could get enough super-famous people involved, they'd make the movie. We got Cameron Diaz, who was great if miscast. And then there was the villain role. The studio wanted Nicolas Cage. I love Nicolas Cage, but our first thought was "There's a wide variety of Nicolas Cages out there—there's *Leaving Las Vegas* Cage, and there's *Wicker Man* Cage. And about a hundred Cages in between. Which Cage are we talking about here?"

But, as bona fide Cage-heads, we were open to it, so we started to have some phone calls with him.

CAGE: I want to play a bald guy but have hair tattooed on my head and big prosthetic lips.

ME: . . . Alright.

CAGE: I wanna do a voice like Edward G. Robinson.

ME: Okay.

CAGE: Actually . . . maybe not the tattooed hair. That's something I might want to do in real life, so it might be weird if I also do it in a movie.

ME: . . . Yeah. That might make it weird.

CAGE: Cool. Let's talk more.

We called the studio and were like, "I'm not sure we're gonna find common ground here. He's coming with weird ideas . . . FOR Nicolas Cage, which is saying something."

The studio came back with "You gotta play this out. Find a way to make it work."

So if you've ever wondered, *"How valuable is Nicolas Cage as a movie star?"* the answer is "So valuable that most movie studios would rather hire him with tattooed hair and fake lips than not hire him at all." Or if you've ever wondered, *"How NOT valuable are you, Seth, as a movie star?"* the answer is "SO not valuable that my presence has to be offset by Nicolas Cage in even the strangest of forms."

Amy Pascal, one of the studio heads, told us that the best way to hash it out would be if we could all just get together at her house and meet face-to-face.

AMY: If we all get along, great. If not, we tried, and we move on. And there's a new idea that he wants to run by you!

ME: Any idea what it is?

AMY: He likes the idea of being a white Bahamian.

ME: A Bohemian? Like a hippie?

AMY: No, A BAHAMIAN. Like . . . from the Caribbean.

ME: Like . . . with an accent?

AMY: I assume, yeah! Otherwise it would be hard to tell he's Bahamian.

Even in 2008, this was a TERRIBLE IDEA. Aside from the fact that it had basically been done in *True Romance*, it seemed to us that it could be very racist.

AMY: There ARE white Bahamians.

ME: I mean, I guess, technically, there must be—

AMY: He said he met one once! Rented scuba equipment from him!

ME: I'm not sure that convinces me.

AMY: Just meet!

A few days later, me and Evan found ourselves driving to Amy's house to have dinner with Nic Cage. I was anxious.

ME: He just better not do the accent. I just . . . I don't know what I'll do.

EVAN: He won't do it! That'd be like auditioning. He's a huge movie star. He's not gonna, like, perform for us.

ME: You don't think so?

EVAN: No way!

ME: Fine. He better not. I truly don't think I'll be able to hold it together if he does.

EVAN: Don't worry. He won't.

We arrived and Nic Cage was already there, and I'm not sure my memory is 100 percent accurate, but I think he was wearing leather pants with pink flames embroidered up the sides of them, which is fucking dope.

We sat down, and within about ten seconds he was on his feet in front of all of us in the middle of the room.

CAGE: Alright, this is how I picture it. You're the Green Hornet, and you're tied up, and I'm dumping pig's blood on you in some, like, creepy voodoo ritual. . . .

Keep in mind there is NO scene in the screenplay that even remotely resembles this, but honestly, maybe there should have been?

Then he did it.

CAGE (IN A BAHAMIAN/JAMAICAN-SOUNDING ACCENT): 'Ello, Green 'Ornet! Wagwan! Why you wear dis mask ting, mon? What dis be, mon? Why you 'iding you face, mon?! I kill you, 'Ornet!! I KILL YOU, 'ORNET!!!!!!!

He stopped and stood there as if he was expecting a rapturous round of applause. There wasn't. Everyone looked to me to say something.

ME: Yeah . . . uh . . . maybe . . . yeah. That's . . . not, like, exactly what we were picturing . . . but, uh . . . maybe?

Nic was visibly devastated by the lack of enthusiasm. He was super-thrown. And it quickly got very awkward. He was REALLY putting himself out there, which I would assume wasn't a big deal for Nic Cage, but he was not immune to the lackluster reaction.

Amy was like, "Let's sit down and eat!" So, we went to her big table, but AS the appetizers were being put out, Nic suddenly got up and was like, "I just realized I gotta go. Sorry. Good to meet you." And he walked out, leaving us at the table.

Amy turned to us with a huge smile on her face, completely oblivious to how awkward it was. "Soo?? Pretty amazing, huh?!"

ME: No! Not amazing! Crazy. We can't do that.

AMY: You have to.

EVAN: What?

AMY: If you wanna make the movie, you gotta cast Nic. He's popular overseas. We've done really well with him. You'll figure out the creative stuff.

EVAN: Will we?!

AMY: If you want to do the movie, you will.

A few days later Nic called and left me a message saying that he could sense that we weren't happy with his take on the character, so he thinks he's not the right guy for the part. At the time I was happy about it, but sometimes I imagine the movie that could have been and think, "Is that worse than what we did, or just way more interesting?"

✿ ✿ ✿

Recently, a movie Nic Cage was attached to star in came across the desk of our production company. We were open to producing the film, and then we got a call from Nic's manager.

NIC'S MANAGER: Nic isn't really sure about you guys. He remembers having a really awkward meeting a few years ago.

ME: Yeah, it was! That happened! We'd be more than willing to sit down and explain everything. I love his work so much, I don't want it to be weird between us!

NIC'S MANAGER: Great. I think that would be good. Nic really wants to talk to you.

He wanted to meet at the Smoke House restaurant in Burbank. We found him seated in the back with his manager. His short beard seemed to be dyed dark brown, which looked kinda bizarre in the most perfect way possible.

I sat down and launched into explaining *The Green Hornet* incident from our perspective and basically apologized profusely for the uncomfortable situation he was dragged into.

ME: I'm so sorry. You got caught in the crosswinds of a hurricane of a movie that was a shitshow in general. It was a fucked-up thing all around, and I'm just sorry that we found ourselves in that room that night.

CAGE: Yeah, alright, it's fine. Look, you're friends with James Franco, right?

ME: . . . Yeah.

CAGE: You saw *Spring Breakers*, right?

I was really confused as to where the fuck this was going.

ME: . . . Yeah. When it came out in theaters.

CAGE: Well . . . did you ever tell him about that meeting we had? About the white Jamaican guy? Is that where he got the idea for the guy in *Spring Breakers*? Did he steal it from me?

ME: Uh . . . no. I don't think I ever mentioned it to him. (I had.) And . . . I don't think he's playing a person of . . . Caribbean origin in that film? (He is definitely not at all.)

CAGE: Because I saw it and I was like, "Fuck! I bet Seth told Franco about it, and then he took it and put it in that movie!"

ME: No. Don't think so. I think there's some Florida rapper that he based it on. Not that meeting we had.

He looked at me like he didn't believe me. Then, just like before, he got up. "Sorry, I gotta go. Nice to see you all."

He and his manager walked away. I turned to Evan.

ME: Did he just meet with us so he could ask us if Franco stole his white Jamaican guy character for *Spring Breakers*? And that's it?

EVAN: Absolutely.

ME: He didn't even believe me when I told him the answer.

EVAN: Nope. He sure didn't.

ME: That's amazing.

❦ ❦ ❦

Although the making of *The Green Hornet* was difficult, you kind of have to delude yourself into thinking you're making a movie that people are going to like no matter what. And you get hopeful. We started testing the movie and it literally tested better than any movie we've ever made. We were excited to go promote the film.

Because Jay Chou was an Asian megastar, they sent us all over Asia to do press. Every airport we landed at had throngs of screaming fans, like, for real. I've never seen anything like it to this day—and I know Zac Efron.

We went to Beijing, where we rode toboggans down a slide alongside the Great Wall of China.

We went to Tokyo, where we ate amazing sushi and I bought weed that came in little Hello Kitty bags.

We went to Seoul, where we ate barbecue and sang kara-oke with women who our hosts had apparently paid to hang out with us.

Singapore was the biggest trip of all. The only real thing I knew about Singapore was that in the nineties, an American did some graffiti there and the punishment was that he was caned, as in whacked by a fucking cane, which is intense. I should also say I learned this fact from a Weird Al song.

The arrival was terrifying. We stepped off the plane, and they took our passports and slipped a little piece of paper inside each one that basically said that if you have drugs on you, they'll execute you, which is a real threat for someone like me. I do, in fact, often have drugs on me, and even though I was pretty sure I didn't at this moment, I've on more than one occasion accidentally brought contraband from one place to another, so this was some high-stakes packing I had just done. Never did the question "Did I accidentally leave a roach in one of my pockets?" have literal life-or-death stakes before, but I'm currently alive so spoiler alert.

We had a premiere, but there are laws against groups of people congregating, so the party was uncomfortable. I remember there was someone from the government there who kept telling people they were allowed to cheer for Jay.

Chewing gum is illegal in Singapore, and it's because someone once stuck a piece to the door of a subway car and it got jammed, which delayed the trains for the next few minutes, and so the only logical thing to do was OUTLAW

FUCKING GUM. I kept being *assured* it wasn't a benevolent dictatorship, it was in fact a thriving democracy, even though I couldn't find one person who had ever voted in their life, so you make the call.

A few months later, I went on Conan O'Brien's show and talked about how culturally different and interesting I found Singapore to be. Singapore did NOT appreciate it. They published a HUGE news story about the shame I brought to Singapore, which I then brought *back* on Conan a few months later to talk about some more.

It's really special when you're able to mock someone, then that person (or country) gets mad, and then you're able to mock THAT, as well. I now call it "the Singapore Cycle," which also sounds like a dope sexual maneuver.

❧ ❧ ❧

The Green Hornet came out, did fine, got pretty bad reviews, and basically became a punch line, which is better than nothing, I guess. Especially for someone who works in comedy.

It's hard to have too much of a takeaway other than we made something that people didn't love, which happens. It's nice when it doesn't; it sucks when it does. Some people did love it, and I'm appreciative of that. Still, it sticks with me, that we spent so much time working on something that so many people took so much joy in deriding, but then I remind myself, "It's fine. Even Nic Cage doesn't like a lackluster reaction."

RHYMIN' AND STEALIN'

The first time I remember hearing any form of rap was in 1988, which means I was six years old. I had a cousin who was about fourteen at the time, and when my family went over for a visit, he looked at me and was like, "Let me show you something cool." We went to his room and he pulled out a record with a colorful jacket and the words "Girls Ain't Nothing But Trouble" written across it. He put it on.

I had actually seen *I Dream of Jeannie* in reruns, so I recognized the theme song when it played. Then a beat dropped under it, Will Smith started rapping over it, I was in.

One of the best byproducts of my job has been that I've gotten to interact and even work with some of my favorite rappers of all time. Musicians are, in general, much crazier than actors, and I think that's because even the most famous actors have to interact with SOME people with regular jobs—film crews, day players, background players. As much as famous actors may try to completely isolate themselves from others, the job doesn't fully allow it. They can get pretty fucking close, like 99 percent, but a full sweep of isolation and social curation is nearly impossible to achieve. But with musicians, it seems they CAN. They appear to be 100 percent insulated. They can handpick every person they interact with every second of the day. They roll deep as FUCK.

It really landed for me the time I tried to get a drink backstage at the Grammys. I had gotten a very random but exciting call that Eminem wanted me to introduce him, Dr. Dre, and Rihanna for a performance of their new song, and when you get that call, you fucking say *yes*. I'd been to a lot of movie award shows at that point, so I thought I knew what to expect, but the Grammys were way different.

Shortly after the opening performance, I was taken backstage. Normally, there's a greenroom where all the presenters and performers and whatnot are milling around, and there's always an open bar so people can have some drinks and dull some nerves while they wait. At the Grammys, every musician essentially had their own greenroom with its own bar, which was completely isolated from all the other celebrity greenrooms. I did not have a greenroom, because I had no idea they were even on the table, so I didn't ask for one. All this is to say, there wasn't an easy way to get a drink. I was so nervous and uncomfortable, I just desperately wanted to inebriate myself in some slight way, and vapes wouldn't be invented for years.

I spotted a big greenroom that said BOB DYLAN, with the doors wide open. There were dozens of people inside, so I was able to sneak in and grab a beer from the bar. I looked for Bob but didn't see him. It would have been amazing to meet him. I'm a huge fan of his, which is kinda like saying,

"I'm a huge fan of pasta," in that who the fuck isn't? There are not a lot of cool Jews to look up to, and he's objectively the top of the list. James Caan being right below him. James Caan is actually a scary Jew, which is almost unheard of. He's in his own lane, Jew-wise.

I finally slipped out with my beer, when a security guard came up to me.

GUARD: **Em wants to say hi before you present. His dressing room is over here.**

ME: **Alright, cool.**

GUARD: **But you can't bring in the beer.**

ME: **I can't? Why?**

GUARD: **Em's sober.**

ME: **Cool.**

GUARD: **So you can't bring it in.**

ME: **I wasn't planning on pouring it in his mouth.**

GUARD: **He can't even be near it.**

This was a level of sobriety that I'd never even heard of. He couldn't even be close to beer in a cup? What would happen?

I didn't want to find out.

I threw out the beer, which upset me, and then had a VERY awkward but thrilling greeting with Eminem and Dr. Dre. (The fact that these guys who I grew up listening to would spend even one moment with me is incredible.)

DRE: **Hope the intro is funny!**

Great, now I was more nervous. I left to go find another drink, which I got from some country musician's dressing room, in the form of a screwdriver, an indisputably disgusting drink.

And then, I saw her—Beyoncé, arm in arm with Gwyneth Paltrow. I don't usually go say hi to other famous people. I generally try to avoid it at all costs, but this was Beyoncé. Or, as my father-in-law calls her, "Bey-onsss." I had to try to say hi.

In retrospect, I approached with too much confidence. I didn't have nearly the reverence I should have. I *should* have gone up to her like you would the queen or that giant bird creature in *Harry Potter* that you have to bow to before you can fly around on it.

I marched up. "Hey, Beyoncé! I'm Seth and—"

A giant arm SWUNG out like a baseball bat and smacked me across the chest so fucking hard I stumbled back and spilled my screwdriver all over myself. I was soaked. Her security had (wisely?) batted me away before I could get close. And at that exact moment, a PA came up to me and said, "Alright, Seth, they're ready for you!"

I was led over to the side of the stage as I tried to figure out if I could hold my arm in a way that covered the screwdriver spill but didn't look too fucking weird. It turns out, I *sorta* could.

Me at the Grammys hiding my spill.

I told my joke, which got a C+ laugh at best, and got the fuck out of there the second I could.

I've gotten to meet Snoop Dogg a couple of times, the first of which was amazing and eye-opening. We have a moment in *This Is the End* where Craig Robinson is serenading a party of people with his staple classic, "Take Yo Panties Off." We thought it would be funny if we had, like, an actual version of the song at the end of the movie, so we asked Snoop Dogg if he would collaborate with Craig, and he said yes.

I arrived at the studio, and soon after, Snoop comes in with, like, four or five people, one of whom is a blunt roller, as in someone whose only job is to roll blunts. He would take a pack of Phillies, open them one by one, empty them all, roll them with weed, and put them back in the Phillies box, then hand them to Snoop, giving him a constant supply.

Snoop wrote the hook with Craig, and after a few hours I was like, "Can you rap a verse?"

SNOOP: **You want me to rap?**

ME: **Yeah, man.**

SNOOP: **Shit. I thought I was just doing the hook.**

ME: **It would be awesome if you could do a verse, too!**

He put his head down and thought for a long moment. Then he looked over to one of his guys, narrowed his gaze . . . and said: "Bring in the hoes."

The guy left, and within thirty seconds he returned with five or six women who were very much dressed like strippers at the start of a routine. The producer blasted the beat, and the women danced and drank while Snoop wrote a rap verse on his BlackBerry.

After about twenty minutes, he was finished writing and gestured to his guy, who escorted the hoes out, vanishing as mysteriously as they had appeared.

This obviously raised a lot of questions.

1. Where were the hoes up till that point? We were not in a big building, and I hadn't seen them before that moment.

2. Why were the hoes there? This was probably the easiest one to figure out. It seemed to be for inspiration. Everyone has their writing process, I guess. I like to drink coffee and sparkling water while I write; Snoop likes to have a team of hoes magically appear and dance around while he writes.

3. Were they there just in case? He didn't think he was gonna be writing any raps, so he, in theory, wouldn't need the hoes' presence. Yet the hoes were present. That seems like a complicated and expensive contingency plan to have in place at all times. A bunch of hoes following you around on the off chance you're asked to write a rap verse. "Who are they?" "Oh, that's just my bus full of muse-hoes in case a song-making opportunity arises!"

4. Why have I been saying "hoes" this whole time? I definitely shouldn't do that.

But, ultimately, my relationship with Kanye West is probably the longest and weirdest.

It all started in 2004. I lived in West Hollywood near Santa Monica and Fairfax, which is meaningless if you don't live in L.A. and uninteresting if you do. One day, I was coming home and there was a dude jogging by my front door who looked exactly like Kanye West. He said, "You're a funny motherfucker," and kept jogging. A few weeks later, I learned I lived right around the corner from one of the most high-end personal trainers in Los Angeles, and Kanye was a client of his. He was there every week.

One morning a few months later, I was unbelievably hungover, and our phone, which is connected to our front gate, rang. Lauren answered.

LAUREN: Hello? Who is this? (Beat.) "Kanye" who? (Beat.) "Kanye East"?

ME: Kanye East? It's Kanye West!

LAUREN: Oh, he's trying to be funny. I get it.

I ran downstairs and opened my front door to see Kanye standing there with a basketball under his arm.

KANYE: Wanna come out and play basketball?

ME: I'm way too hungover. I'll throw up all over the place.

Kanye hung his head and walked off, sadly.

It's a bummer to have to say no to people when you're a fan. Once, we ran into Diddy in Sonoma and he asked me and Lauren if we wanted to go hot-air ballooning with him the next morning, but we had to say no because we were scouting locations for our wedding. We both still talk about how insane and awkward that would have been, and we wish we could have experienced it. I can't decide if he'd have been really brazen or endearingly scared of the heights and the fire.

I'd seen Kanye fairly regularly over the years, but it all came to a head the day we saw the music video for "Bound 2."

We were filming *The Interview* in Vancouver, and Kanye was on tour. He kept canceling his shows and we were kinda pissed. Then "Bound 2" came out. The video itself is, in a word, terrible. It's basically Kanye and Kim writhing around on a motorcycle in front of a green screen while images of mountains and skies are superimposed behind them. The production budget appears to have been somewhere in the neighborhood of $27.68.

It was obvious someone was gonna make fun of it, so we were like: Can we do it sooner and better than other people? Sooner probably being the more important of the two? We bet that we could.

If the original video came out at 10 A.M., by noon the same day we were filming our version. At first, we were just gonna make fun of a little bit of it, but Franco was like, "If we're gonna do this, we should do the entire thing shot for shot. Let's not half-ass it. Let's just fucking do it if we're gonna do it."

So we did it.

Making viral videos is impossible, in that you don't actually know what's gonna go viral. Marketing people in Hollywood always think they can control it—they're always like, "We'll do this video of you guys being funny, and it'll go viral." But it never does. This was not like that. The whole time we were making it, we were like, "There's zero percent chance it doesn't go everywhere instantly. It will go viral." And it very much did. A few weeks after it came out, an eighty-year-old woman came up to me and recognized me as "the guy from the motorcycle video." I remember thinking that it was maybe the most popular thing I had ever been a part of.

About six months later, I was in New York with Lauren to film a tiny guest spot on the first episode of Jimmy Fallon's *Tonight Show*. We had just bought a bunch of dessert and brought it back to the Mercer Hotel, where we were staying. We stopped in the lobby to get some plates and cutlery and shit, when I heard a voice from behind me.

"Yo!!"

We turned around, and there was Kanye West. I was nervous at first. I'd clowned him pretty hard and pretty well. It really landed. Thank god, he wasn't mad.

ME: Yo!!!!!! Hey, man, first off, I'm sorry if you were offended by the video or anything! I love the song and the album so much!

KANYE: No! It's fine! I loved it! Honestly, I think you were the only ones who actually got how stupid and bad our video was supposed to be.

I'm still not sure this is true, but, sure, I'll take it.

ME: Phew! Yeah! I thought so! Again, you know it's done out of love. I'm such a huge fan. I actually kept trying to see your show in Vancouver, but you canceled it twice!

KANYE: Oh shit, yeah. Uh . . . you wanna hear some new music I've been working on?

LAUREN: Uh . . . yeah. We'd love to.

KANYE: Come out to my van.

LAUREN: Your . . . van?

KANYE: I got a big van!

Vans have swept Hollywood recently. A lot of motherfuckers get these big-ass Mercedes vans that they deck out into mobile offices. It reminds me of John Hurt in *Contact,* floating around space, teleconferencing. I don't have a van, but if I did have a van, people wouldn't think it was strange, which shows how weird van culture really is. When I was a kid, people who owned vans were creepy grossos who might kidnap children, and I'd prefer to keep it that way.

We go out to his big van, which essentially looks like the

first-class cabin of a commercial airplane, except with more LED lighting. He pulls out a laptop, plugs it into the AUX cable, and brings up an iTunes playlist of about twenty songs.

KANYE: **Alright, so I only have the beats and some of them don't have hooks, so I'll just fill in everything else, okay?**

ME: Uh . . . yeah. Sure.

He hits play, and the beat kicks in loud.

KANYE: **Alright, and I start rapping here, and I'm like: Bip bita BOP and a boom bita BAP, and everyone goes, THANK YOU (you, you, you, you). And then I come back in again rapping like: Boom whapa BAM and PA whapa BAM, and then I say, THANK YOU (you, you, you, you). And then Frank Ocean will come in here and be like: Baaaa ba boooooooooooo.**

I've been in a few situations where rappers play you their music, and it's always incredibly awkward. I never really know what to do. Do I look them in the eye? Is that too personal? If I just look at the floor, will it seem like I don't like it? How much do I bob my head? What if I'm bobbing on the ones and threes instead of the twos and fours? It's generally strange, but this was WAYYYYY stranger. Even though there was plenty of space in the van, we were, like, knee to knee. He was inches from our faces at times.

He finished the song, and me and my wife applauded.

LAUREN: **That was AWESOME! So great. So cool. When it's done it's gonna be amazing.**

KANYE: **Alright, thanks. Here's the NEXT song!**

And then he did the same thing to the next song, and the next song, and the seventeen songs after that. All in all, we were in the van for about two and a half hours as Kanye gave us a private performance. It was quite incredible.

Then, somehow, it got even weirder.

After the last song, he opened another file on his computer and turned the screen toward us.

KANYE: Check it out.

There was a drawing of a voluptuous tiger/lady/creature. Like if Kim Kardashian was cast in the movie *Cats*.

KANYE: This is my new shit. It's a movie.

LAUREN: What's it about?

KANYE: Let me show you . . .

He then, for the next forty minutes or so, took us through the storyboards for an entire movie about these sexy cat creatures.

KANYE: They find this tree, and it's, like, sexy, and there's fruit on the tree, you get that? You get the analogy? Like the Bible, but with these sexy cats. And they're all going to be, like, really sexy. And it'll play on this . . .

He pulled up a rendering of what looked like a movie theater, but instead of just one screen in front of the audience, there was another one above them and four surrounding them.

KANYE: It'll feel like you're IN the movie, actually surrounded by these sexy cat bitches.

ME: Like 3D?

KANYE: No way, man! 3D is fucking LAME. Nobody wants to wear those stupid glasses! You wanna go to a movie and look like a fucking moron? Fuck no.

He had a point.

About a year later, his next album came out, and not one of the songs he played us was on it.

Randomly, around that time, I got a phone call from Kanye, who was about to get married to Kim.

KANYE: I'm having an engagement party in Versailles, France,

and I thought it would be funny if I sang "Bound 2" at the party and you and Franco came out on a motorcycle when I sang it. . . . You kinda writhe around and . . . then it'll be awkward, and you'll just be up there, and then I'm rapping at my own engagement party with two shirtless guys who aren't friends with anyone there. . . . Maybe not.

It was nice that his idea evaporated as it was entering the atmosphere, like a little meteor. Because if it hadn't, I definitely would have done it, and it would have been a glorious disaster.

I don't have any real deep insight into Kanye and his current state of being or mindset other than to say I really love his music and my interactions with him have been lovely. But I'm sure a lot of people have said the same about a lot of people who have made incredibly shitty comments. I recently read about a phenomenon where everyone assumes *their* actions are based on love and the actions of those they disagree with are based on hate. I don't think Kanye is hateful. I think he is grasping and struggling to make his way through life, and as painless as his experience seems like it should be, there's no pain more painful than your own pain, and that goes for everyone, even Kanye. That said, I really wish he would shut the fuck up about all this political bullshit. That doesn't help anything.

✾ ✾ ✾

POSTSCRIPT: A few years ago, a guy came up to me on the street and was like, "Oh, man, a while back I was at the Grammys with my buddy who looks just like you! You were there, too! You introduced Eminem! Anyway, at the end of the night a security guard came up to my buddy and handed him a harmonica and said, 'Bob's a big fan of yours.'"

I'm only including this story on the off chance that the person who got the harmonica is reading this book. PLEASE GIVE ME THAT SHIT! You've had a good run with it! Let me have it. I'll give you something else cool. I'll make you four vases. Thanks.

HACKS

I t all started with a joke.

"These TV reporters, a lot of them interview the worst people in the world—bin Laden, Qaddafi. Wouldn't it save everyone a lot of trouble if they just killed the person they were interviewing? Someone interviewed Hitler before the Holocaust. . . . Just shoot him!"

That's really where the seed of the idea for our film *The Interview* started, but the thing that made it bloom was an obsession with North Korea. Me and Evan were just so fascinated by it. It's unique in the world: an isolated country whose leader has godlike status, its citizens shut off from any information that might lead them to think otherwise.

During the writing process, Kim Jong Il died and was succeeded by his son Kim Jong Un, who was even more compelling to us. He was around our age, and from what we were reading, he also had a lot of the same interests. He loved American movies, television shows, basketball. He was into fancy sports cars, which would make someone a total douche if they weren't also super-short, which he is, so it's fine. We heard he loved Ryan Seacrest. . . .

He had this insane and hilarious mythology about him. They said he could golf a perfect game every time; that he had assassinated a unicorn by hand; that he never went to the bathroom, because he had no butthole—he had no need for one, as his body ran so efficiently there was no waste.

Knowing everything we do about celebrities—how vain they are, how easily manipulated and impressed they are, how much they like OTHER famous people—we realized: If an American celebrity came to North Korea and met Kim Jong Un in person, they'd probably be shocked to find themselves really liking the guy.

So, in the film *The Interview,* a very stupid American talk-show host named Dave Skylark finds out that Kim Jong Un is a fan of his. In an attempt to get ratings, he secures an interview with Kim. Soon after, he's approached by the CIA to actually kill Kim. Skylark sees this as an even greater opportunity for fame and agrees. But when he gets to North Korea, he finds that he and Kim Jong Un not only get along, they have a lot in common. Both famous, both misunderstood and isolated. They become friends. It's then revealed that Kim Jong Un is manipulating the incredibly stupid American for his own benefit. But we'll get back to that later. . . .

Some movies are really hard to get made. *Superbad* took over a decade. *Sausage Party, Pineapple Express, This Is the End,* each took six to seven years, all because studios just couldn't wrap their heads around how any of these movies could possibly make money.

The Interview was different. After the FIRST draft was handed in, Amy Pascal called: "If you can get James Franco in this movie, we'll make it." Alright. That was easy. We sent him the script, he said yes, and we were greenlit with only ONE note from the studio.

"In your movie, you made up a dictator. Would it be funnier if it was actually Kim Jong Un? Like you guys did in *This Is the End*?"

We were like, "Yeah. Sure."

Aside from me almost getting killed by a tiger (page 203), the filming was largely uneventful—in a good way. After we were finished, the shit really hit the fan.

We edited a cut relatively quickly and did a test screening. The numbers were wildly encouraging. It was one of the highest-testing films we've ever had. Audiences seemed to really like it.

We cut a trailer, and in June 2014, it was released. About two weeks later, the UN representative from North Korea sent the following letter to the secretary general of the UN:

General, I have the honour to transmit herewith a copy of the statement released by the spokesperson for the Ministry of Foreign Affairs of the Democratic People's Republic of Korea with regard to a film made in the United States of America whose plot involves insulting and assassinating the supreme leadership of the Democratic People's Republic of Korea (see annex).

To allow the production and distribution of such a film on the assassination of an incumbent Head of a sovereign State should be regarded as the most undisguised sponsoring of terrorism as well as an act of war.

The United States authorities should take immediate and appropriate actions to ban the production and distribution of the aforementioned film; otherwise, it will be fully responsible for encouraging and sponsoring terrorism.

I should be grateful if you would have the present letter and its annex circulated as a document of the General Assembly, under agenda item 110, and of the Security Council.

Ja Song Nam
Ambassador
Permanent Representative

A couple days after that, the Korean Central News Agency released a statement from the country's foreign minister, who said that the North Korean government promised a "merciless" retaliation against the United States if *The Interview* was released, calling the film itself an "act of war." They went on to say the film was a "wanton act of terror" that was the work of "gangster moviemakers," which is hands down the coolest thing a foreign dictator can call you.

We weren't that surprised. North Korea had a real history of releasing wildly inflammatory statements, so it was on brand.

We were summoned to meet with Michael Lynton, who was the head of Sony. We'd dealt with him a bit on *The Green Hornet,* and I was generally terrified of him. He was a dude in his mid-fifties, relatively fit, red skin, large horns, a tail, hooves, and a legion of screaming demons flanking him at all times.

We got to his office, where we were introduced to a representative from the RAND Corporation, a think tank that weighs in on risk assessment, among many other things. The dude from RAND had compiled a report.

RAND Dude: Well, North Korea does not seem happy.

Me: Will they be even more unhappy when they actually see the movie?

RAND DUDE: From what we can tell, they likely already hacked into Sony's servers and watched the film, which is why they issued such a strong response.

LYNTON: What's the most egregious part, you think?

RAND DUDE: Well, the characterization is a big issue, because it is quite accurate. From his hobbies to his interpersonal relationships with his father and brother, it'll really hit home for him.

We did do a lot of research, so this was nice to hear.

LYNTON (TALKING OVER SCREAMING–DEMON ARMY): Okay, what else might be a problem?

RAND DUDE: I notice you used a lot of actual imagery of Kim Jong Il and Kim Il Sung, Un's father and grandfather.

ME: Yes. We cleared all the actual imagery that we legally could.

RAND DUDE: Well, they're not gonna like that at all.

LYNTON: Okay . . . maybe we can do something about that. What else?

RAND DUDE: Well, obviously, the ending is an issue. You VERY graphically explode Kim Jong Un's head, and since he's viewed as God, it's exploding God's head, and, well, you see how that could be . . . problematic. All I can say is, protect yourselves. They already likely hacked into your systems once; they'll probably try to do it again as you get closer to release.

Over the next couple months, as we finished the film, the studio asked us to make a series of annoying but mostly benign changes.

The first was taking the word "Sony" off the movie, so as not to remind people that the movie was ultimately made by a Japanese company, due to Japan's terrible history with Korea. I'm not sure if they thought people were just gonna forget that Columbia Pictures is owned by Sony, but nowhere in the film or its marketing materials does it say, "A Sony Picture," which is probably a rare distinction for Sony Pictures.

Also, there are little pins worn by every North Korean character in the movie, with Kim Jong Il and Kim Il Sung on them, as well as countless other images of them on propaganda posters in the background of shots. The studio insisted on going in and EVER SO SLIGHTLY digitally altering them so it was not *technically* them we were showing. Me and Evan got really mad about it—then we saw the first shots come back from visual effects and we literally couldn't tell the difference, so we didn't make a big deal out of it.

The last thing was the death.

Lynton called us. "Can you not kill him?"

ME: It's kind of baked in there. Unless you want to spend a lot of money reshooting a new ending.

The studio NEVER wants to spend a lot of money on anything, so it's always a good thing to bring up budget when you're not into an idea.

LYNTON: Can you cut around it?

ME: Not really.

Basically we agreed to tone the shot down a bit, which wasn't that hard to do, because it was quite toned UP when we filmed it.

Whenever there's something that we fear might be watered down by the studio, we go WAYYYYY overboard on set so we have a lot of room to negotiate. We knew that graphically killing Kim Jong Un would very likely become a debated point while we were editing, so we shot it in the most explicit way imaginable, giving us something to pull back on.

We had the practical-effects team build a realistic replica

of Randall Park's head, in character as Kim. The head had layers of wax and fake bone that perfectly replicated what was inside an actual head. We used a super-high-speed camera and blasted the wax head with flamethrowers, causing the layers to melt, one after the other. Once it was just a flaming skeleton, a small explosive was detonated, blowing up what was left of his head.

"We want it to be the face melting in *Raiders*, followed up by the head explosion from *Scanners*" were likely the exact words we used when explaining it to our crew.

After a LOT of back and forth, we agreed to slightly alter the shot so you don't see quite as much face melting before the head exploding. It got VERY granular. We literally created hundreds of versions of the shot as we tried to arrive at a consensus.

In October, Kazuo Hirai, the chairman of Sony, weighed in with his feedback to Amy over (now hacked) email: "I've given this a lot of thought and would like to go ahead with a variation of version 337. . . . It would be much appreciated if you could push them a bit further as you mentioned in your email. Also, please ensure that this does not make it into the international version of the release."

The studio had started making their own shots at this point, and we didn't think their version worked. I wrote back: "We will make it less gory. There are currently four burn marks on his face. We will take out three of them, leaving only one. We will reduce the flaming hair by 50 percent. . . . The head explosion can't be more obscured than it is because we honestly feel that if it's any more obscured you won't be able to tell it's exploding, and the joke won't work. Do you think this will help? Is it enough?"

After a few back and forths, I wrote: "This is it!!! We removed the fire from the hair and the entire secondary wave of head chunks. Please tell us this is over now. Thanks so much!!"

It was. We had settled on a version and we were heading into the months leading up to release on relatively the same page. Except for one.

Me and Evan took the RAND Corporation's warning seriously. We avoided the Sony servers at all costs, as we'd been told they'd likely *already* been hacked, and hired our own people to help secure our networks. Sony, it would seem, did not.

Although it didn't become public until November 24, the Sony hack actually happened on November 21. I'm sure a lot of people wondered, *What was Michael Lynton doing the moment he found out about the hack?* And by a crazy stroke of coincidence, I actually know what he was doing. He was in the Rita Hayworth building on the Sony lot, sitting down in front of Sony's international-TV-and-movie-distribution partners, conducting a Q and A with me.

Halfway through the Q and A, a security guard came in and whispered in Lynton's ear, and he excused himself for a few minutes, during which time I had to tread water with Sony's international-distribution partners. It was sweaty as fuck, but what really stood out to me was that when Lynton returned, he looked like he had seen a ghost. He was pale, clammy, and obviously not in the mood to be mid–Q and A with *me* of all people. It would be like if George Bush was reading that pet goat book *to* Osama bin Laden when he found out about 9/11 and then had to keep reading.

The next few weeks were . . . chaotic. The press packaged the contents of various emails into stories that were blasted everywhere throughout December. I try not to be too judgmental of anyone, including journalists, but there was some shit that went down during the hack that was debatable.

Imagine you had a safe with your secrets in it—secret ideas and projects that you were working on in hopes of selling them to the world. Things of both emotional and monetary value. Imagine those things were stolen and given to, say, *The Hollywood Reporter*. And imagine *The Hollywood Reporter*, instead of saying, "Oh, man, you were robbed, that's too bad! You were the victim of a crime. Let's not add insult to injury! Here are your possessions back!" said, "Oh fuck! You got robbed! Well, we're gonna go through ALL THE CONTENTS OF WHAT WAS STOLEN from you, and we're gonna take the best shit, and we're gonna sell that shit ourselves, motherfucker!"

At least, that's kinda what happened. Sony was robbed, and the media took the contents of that robbery and sold it off to the public bit by bit, which wasn't necessarily how I thought that would go down but ultimately shouldn't be that surprising. There was some juicy shit in there, so it was hard to resist.

Amy Pascal had sent some racially insensitive jokes to Scott Rudin, and the media was all over it. At least the Amy part of it. Nobody seemed to give a shit about Scott.

Despite all this, the movie was supposed to open well and was tracking for a thirty-million-dollar-plus weekend, which is fucking great. Like the kind of thing that might never happen for an actor or writer or director ever in their career, and I wasn't taking that for granted at all. It's hard to make a movie that really resonates with audiences, and it seemed we had made one.

The next day, we were going to have the Los Angeles premiere. We'd settled on a decent middle ground on the head blowing up, but Lynton was getting cold feet. The morning of the premiere, I was called into his office. The flames licked around his giant throne made of bones.

LYNTON: Look, we're going to put together a version of the death where the whole thing is obscured by fire, so you don't actually see anything. And also, because of the hack, the press now knows that there's been some back and forth about this, so if you are asked about this, I need you to say you wanted to do it.

ME: But I don't.

LYNTON: Yeah. But it's best for the movie if you just say you do.

Changing the movie in a way you think is bad and then lying about it publicly isn't usually a good thing, never mind the *best* thing. It's usually a fucking terrible and dumb thing. I hate lying to the press in interviews. I pretty much reverse engineer a lot of my career decisions knowing that one day I'll be promoting my work, and I don't wanna feel like I'm lying to anyone. I don't wanna *trick* people into seeing my shit. I wanna make shit they wanna see, and then talking about it is easy. I know one day I'll be sitting across from Howard Stern and he'll grill the shit out of me for everything I've done since seeing him last, and I truly want to be able to speak openly and honestly about my life and career choices. So this seemed like it was gonna fuck all that up. But the chairman of the studio releasing your movie is a hard dude to say no to, so I said yes. We'd screen the movie as it currently was at the premiere that night, but tomorrow we'd change it to ready it for release.

That night, we had the L.A. premiere at the United Artists Theater downtown. It was pouring rain, which always makes L.A. feel like the movie *Se7en*. In other words, a wonderful vibe. We took pictures on the red carpet but didn't actually talk to journalists, and I vaguely remember running away from someone from *Variety* when they tried to interview me.

Halfway through the movie, I took two large capsules filled with MDMA crystals. By the time the movie ended, they were kicking in HARD. We went to the top floor of the hotel for a party, and the mood was oddly good. The movie had played well, and even though there was a tornado of shit swirling around us, for a moment it seemed like we were in the calm eye of the storm. Then the head of visual effects for Sony came up to me and Evan.

VFX Guy: I got the new version of the shot!

Me: Huh? What?

VFX Guy: You know. The conversation you and Michael had this morning? About the new version of the shot? I have it.

Evan: Where?

VFX Guy: On my phone. We gotta approve tonight.

Me: And we gotta approve it on your phone?

VFX Guy: Yep! We have to deliver the movie to theaters tomorrow. We have to approve this now.

We went into the bathroom of one of the hotel rooms, and I was rolling my goddamn ass off. My face was sweating. My body was tingling. With every breath, a wave of euphoria swept away the anxiety that was fighting to take over.

The VFX Guy held up his phone and we watched the shot, which essentially was just CG flames rolling over the frame for, like, fifteen seconds. You really couldn't see anything at all. And it was on a phone, circa 2014.

Evan: Can we shorten the shot?

VFX Guy: What do you mean?

Evan: Well, the length of the shot is what it is because

we're holding to show his head explode, but without that, there's no reason to hold the shot for so long. It's just kind of weird.

VFX Guy: No, we can't open editorial again. Just VFX.

Me and Evan looked at each other. It just sucked so bad. It's an odd feeling when you're on tons of MDMA and something really shitty is happening. Your body doesn't quite know how to compute it. I started seeing spots as my torso went numb.

Me: I'm gonna talk to Michael tomorrow. I don't think we can do this.

I emailed Lynton that night, saying we needed to talk in the morning—FIRST thing in the morning.

When I woke up, I realized maybe I should have made the meeting second or even third thing in the morning, because I was still incredibly high. I'd say about 64 percent high. But the meeting was set. I showered and took a cab to Sony because I honestly didn't think I could drive. I was nervous when I got there, so I stopped at the Coffee Bean to get a big cup of coffee, thinking that might keep my sober edge sharp. I chugged the coffee and hurried to Lynton's office, but the mixture of the caffeine and my heart pumping from being nervous made the remnants of the MDMA start to race through my veins. As I walked up to the desk outside his office, I found myself 100 percent high again.

Me: Hi. It's Seth for Michael.

Assistant: You can head in. He'll be with you in a second.

I went into his HUGE office and sat across from the empty desk. I felt like I was in the movie *Network*, about to be yelled at for meddling with the forces of nature. I thought to myself: *Alright, maybe he'll leave me waiting in here for a bit, and I can chill out, take a few deep breaths, maybe drink some water, and by then I'll be a bit less high*—and then he walked in.

LYNTON: **Yes?**

ME: **Look . . . I can't do it. I can't lie. Either we leave the shot how it is, which I already don't love, or we can change it. But I'm not gonna pretend that it was my idea, and if anyone asks me, I'm gonna be honest and say you made us change it.**

He stared at me for a while with a look that made me think, *Has this motherfucker had people killed? He kinda* looks *like he has. And if he has, is this a killable offense?*

Then he said . . . "I understand."

ME: **That's it?**

LYNTON: **Yep. That's it.**

ME: **. . . Alright.**

Everything went WAYYYY worse from there on out.

I went to New York to start doing the final week of promotion, and reviews started to come out, and they were pretty shitty. There's nothing more fun than reading a terrible review of your movie in *USA Today* on your phone as you walk into an interview with a journalist from *USA Today*. "Here's my stamp of approval on your trash-talking of my film! I condone this outlet and their message!"

Meanwhile, the media kept delving more and more into the hacked emails and finding more and more stuff that they deemed publishable. Hilariously, the original shot of the head blowing up was released online by Gawker, which I could appreciate the irony of in a Morissette-ian way. But it's also never great when the grand-finale shot of your film is released online by a website a week before the movie is supposed to come out.

On December 17, we were supposed to have a New York

premiere, and I was in a car on my way to do Fallon. As we got close to 30 Rock, the news reported that there were threats of violence against theaters that showed the movie. All of a sudden, the idea of doing a lip-synch battle to promote the film seemed wrong. The premiere was canceled that night, and I was flooded with calls for comment. I didn't know what to say—which is an admission I should probably arrive at more often—so I said nothing.

The press was split in a lot of ways at this point, but there was a ton of "don't poke the bear" messaging being thrown our way, which is crazy. I agree, don't poke a bear. But dictators aren't bears. Bears are animals that don't know any better than to follow their natural instincts. Dictators are pieces of shit who deserve ridicule. A lot of people I knew from Hollywood were giving me advice on what to say: "Pull the movie!" "Tell Kim Jong Un to go fuck himself and get behind free speech!" "Ask the government to get involved!"

The best advice came from Sacha Baron Cohen, who of all the people in the world was probably in the best position to understand how to navigate this. After *Borat,* he, too, had alienated an entire country, Kazakhstan, and although they didn't have nearly good enough technology to hack a studio, the situation was comparable. "Say nothing. Just keep your fucking mouth shut. If you want more attention, talk. If you want less, say nothing at all. If you talk, you give them more to write about. More quotes. If you just shut up, there's nothing to report."

I said nothing, and of all the shit I did throughout that time, it was one of the smarter things. But it's clearly advice I've since stopped listening to.

Sony didn't really communicate anything with me directly at that point, so I just went back to L.A. While I was on the plane, they announced that they were pulling the movie from its planned theatrical release.

I landed and was pissed. I called Lynton.

ME: **You specifically promised me you wouldn't pull the movie. You knew all this was going to happen.**

LYNTON: **Nobody could have known this was going to happen.**

ME: **Actually, the RAND Corporation, who you hired, knew this was going to happen, and they told us as much about five months ago. I was there! That's why I hired cybersecurity, and I wasn't hacked!**

LYNTON: **Look, right now you feel we're making a mistake. But you're alone in that feeling. Everyone I've talked to feels we're making the right decision. Industry-wide, it's being viewed as the wisest choice.**

ME: **I really think it's wrong, and I'm gonna come out and say it, unless we work on a way to let the theaters that want to show the film be allowed to show it and we find a streaming platform to release it before the end of the year.**

LYNTON: **Again, I understand that right now you feel like we're making a mistake and new actions need to be taken, but let's just wait a day. Tomorrow, President Obama is giving his year-end press conference. Let's see if this comes up, see what he says, and move forward from there.**

This was incredibly ominous for one big reason: Lynton knew President Obama. He was a huge supporter of his, and from the way he was talking, it felt like he had some sort of inside track on what the president was going to say. And it *really* seemed like he thought whatever President Obama was going to say would support him and his decisions, which was terrifying to me.

The next morning we all gathered in our office, which was

actually on the Sony lot, and turned on the TV just as the press conference was about to start. Part of me didn't really think the president would even mention us. It was the year-end press conference; surely there'd be more important things to talk about.

Nope. It was the first question. And the second question. And a bunch of ones after that.

REPORTER: I'll start on North Korea.... Did Sony make the right decision in pulling the movie, or does that set a dangerous precedent when faced with this kind of situation?

PRESIDENT OBAMA: Sony is a corporation. It suffered significant damage. There were threats against its employees. I am sympathetic to the concerns that they faced.

We were devastated. It seemed as though Lynton had pulled some magic trick and gotten the president of the United States himself to support his argument. But then he continued . . .

PRESIDENT OBAMA: Having said all that, yes, I think they made a mistake.

We literally exploded in applause. He went on . . .

PRESIDENT OBAMA: We cannot have a society in which some dictator someplace can start imposing censorship here in the United States. Because if somebody is able to intimidate folks out of releasing a satirical movie, imagine what they start doing when they see a documentary that they don't like or news reports that they don't like. Or even worse, imagine if producers and distributors and others start engaging in self-censorship because they don't want to offend the sensibilities of somebody whose sensibilities probably need to be offended. So that's not who we are. That's not what America is about. Again, I'm sympathetic that Sony, as a private company, was worried about liabilities and this and that and the other. I wish they had

spoken to me first. I would have told them, "Do not get into a pattern in which you're intimidated by these kinds of criminal attacks." . . . I think it says something interesting about North Korea that they decided to have the state mount an all-out assault on a movie studio because of a satirical movie. . . . I love Seth and I love James, but the notion that that was a threat to them, I think gives you some sense of the kind of regime we're talking about here.

He put Sony on blast. Lynton called a few hours later to figure out how to get the movie to theaters that wanted it and to find a streaming platform to partner with.

It premiered on Google Play at the end of December. And that's when even *more* reviews started to come out. In what is definitely the most revealing thing about me, the piece of all this that I still carry around is that the film was negatively received for the most part.

The question of "Was it all worth it for *this* movie?" became a popular one. If critics had liked it more, would it have been more worthwhile? Because it didn't align with their taste, it wasn't? That conversation was frustrating, and frankly really painful. But getting shitty reviews always hurts. I'm not sure if critics don't realize how much their words can hurt someone or they just don't care? Maybe they see brutal criticism as a painful but necessary part of our lives, like going to the dentist? All this is to say that it actually hurts.

But what hurt much more than critics talking shit was other comedians talking shit.

I try not to publicly malign the work of other comedians (unless I genuinely dislike them on a personal level), probably because I'm so sensitive to it that the idea of subjecting anyone else to it seems crazy. But around the release of the movie, and in the months following, people I really respected started mocking the movie—not just what happened with it; they literally were saying it was shitty. A joke Amy Poehler and Tina Fey made at the Golden Globes that year was particularly painful, not only because I look up to them so much but because I knew they were right and that the movie itself wasn't as good as it could have been.

For the weeks surrounding the release, the studio demanded we all have armed security with us twenty-four hours a day. I didn't like it. It made me uncomfortable. And the whole time we were like, "Do we really need these guys? This is silly. Aren't we just drawing more attention to the whole situation? Like North Korea is gonna send an assassin to West Hollywood?"

Then one day in early January, I came outside to walk to the coffee shop, expecting to see my guard, but he was gone. Vanished, nowhere to be found. At first I was like, *Was he taken out? Is this an attack?* I called Evan.

ME: Is your guard still there?

EVAN: No! I just went outside! He's gone!

ME: I guess . . . we're not in danger anymore?

EVAN: I guess not?

ME: Did the studio call to say they were relieving the guy of duty or whatever?

EVAN: No. He's just . . . gone.

ME: . . . I'm starting to miss that guy.

EVAN: Me, too. I felt so safe with him around.

In the following weeks, I worried that the movie would be on me like a stain forever. That people would never look at me the same way again, and that maybe people just wouldn't think I was funny anymore. What I really learned, though, was how fucking fast people forget shit and move on. Once again, an inflated sense of self-importance ultimately made the fallout not as bad as I thought it would be. By mid-January, I was in San Francisco rehearsing for the Steve Jobs movie. Kate Winslet turned to me and was like, "What was with that whole North Korea mess, dear? Did anything ever come of that?"

ME: I guess not.

Amy stepped down that February and set up a production company. She always joked that if she wasn't the head of the studio, she'd be in our offices—the "schoolhouse," as it was known on the lot. Turns out it wasn't a joke. She kicked us out of our offices to set up her own. There was a news story about how she had to let them air out for a week to get rid of the weed smell, which seems like an exaggeration of at least a day or two.

We were moved into one of Adam Sandler's storage rooms. For real. We never got full ownership of one of the closets in the office, and every few days, someone from Happy Madison Productions would come into our reception area to grab toilet paper.

Since stepping down, Amy's won two Oscars and been nominated for another two.

Michael Lynton, who always claimed there was no way he could have seen any of this coming—even though I saw him warned about it months earlier—left the company soon after and is now on the board of Snapchat. So, the next time some high school senior sends his girlfriend dick pics, Lynton will be cashing a check. He also remains the Lord of the Underworld and its Flaming Dominions of Torment (L.U.F.D.T. for short).

✿ ✿ ✿

Cut to 2018. A charismatic yet completely moronic TV-show host (who is also president, but I'm sure critics would have said that was way too broad for our film) gets an invite to go to North Korea. He accepts with the intention of showing Kim Jong Un who's boss. Trump had always been hard on Kim. He would make fun of him, calling him "Rocket Man" and stupid shit like that. But once he got there . . . he actually liked him! When he got back from his trip, he had this to say about his meeting:

TRUMP (IN STUPID, DUMB FUCKING VOICE): **When I did it, and I was really being tough, and so was he, and we'd go back and forth, and then we fell in love. No really. He wrote me beautiful letters. And they're great letters. We fell in love.**

He fell in love with the motherfucker. In the movie, the stupid talk-show host eventually finds out that Kim was tricking him and exposes him as a fraud. Trump hasn't quite gotten there yet.

In early 2020, after there were rumors that Kim Jong Un had died following a botched surgery, he resurfaced, and Trump couldn't have been more psyched. "I'm glad to see he's back and well!"

I shudder when I think about what would have happened if Trump was president when all this shit went down. He'd have sent my fucking head to North Korea in a box in exchange for some beautiful letters.

As strange a time as it all was, there were a lot of bright spots. Lauren couldn't have been more supportive and wonderful. In the midst of the mayhem, I got an email from Russell Crowe, who I'd only met a couple times, inviting me to his ranch in Australia to hide if I needed to. I said no, but it always struck me as nice. George Clooney tried to get all the heads of the major studios to sign a letter in solidarity with Sony and the film. None of them would sign it, but I appreciated the attempt. The fact that Clooney spent even one afternoon thinking of me is flattering.

Every once in a while, I'll be flipping channels and see the movie playing on FX or Comedy Central. At one point, this was the most controversial film in the world—people thought they could die if they screened it. And now it's playing on basic cable at 3 P.M., and it's brought to you by Charmin, which is a superior toilet paper in both thickness and softness, so I take that as a win.

TIGERS!!!!!!!!

In our extensive research about North Korea, one of the most interesting tidbits that stuck out to us was that there are wild tigers there, and it seemed like it could potentially be interesting to include that in *The Interview* in some way.

We had a scene where the CIA is trying to drop a little remote-controlled missile with a poison strip in it in a field outside Kim Jong Un's fortress, and my character has to sneak into the field to retrieve it. We thought it would be funny if I encountered a tiger, which attacks me and is ultimately killed by the missile that I was sent to retrieve.

At first, the obvious idea was to use a CGI tiger. The movie *Life of Pi* had recently come out, and the fake tiger in that movie was pretty fucking great. But we very quickly deduced that we didn't have nearly the budget to make a convincing fake tiger. So the idea came up to use a real tiger.

If you've ever made a movie or TV show or know anyone

who has, the phrase "children and animals" comes up a lot as the two things you want to avoid filming if you can. And there's good reason: They're dangerous and difficult and time-consuming.

Once I did a photo shoot where I had a small monkey on my shoulder and was fucking BLOWN AWAY when I met the monkey, because it was MARCEL! The monkey from *Friends*! This was a famous-ass monkey. Honestly, this monkey had a better résumé than I do, from both a quality and box-office standpoint. This was as professional a monkey as you could ask for. I was psyched.

"Oh, man! Can I hug him?"

"No. Don't make any sudden movements. Don't raise your voice. Try not to laugh too loud. If he's startled, he may try to bite your nose off."

Fucking Christ. The headline that I had my nose bit off by the monkey from *Friends* was not really something I wanted to see, mostly because it for sure would have made me laugh if it happened to another celebrity.

And a tiger, on the grand scale of animals you don't want to work with, is pretty fucking high. And, as with children, the animals themselves often aren't the worst part. It's their parents/owners.

But we liked the joke, so we plowed forward.

We were filming in Vancouver and were told that the tiger itself had to come from Canada, because I guess getting a tiger over the border is hard, which is probably a good thing. There was really only one option: hiring a tiger wrangler from Calgary named Randy.

We were sent some photos of his tigers, and they were, in fact, big-ass fucking tigers. He sent us a link to a video of him using a big fishing rod–type thing with a lure, having the tigers run around, jump up on boxes, wrestle with him—you know, crazy tiger dude–type shit. The guy himself looked and dressed kinda like Indiana Jones . . . if Indiana Jones had gained sixty pounds and was not as attractive as Harrison Ford in the first place. If you've seen *Tiger King*, you get the general vibe of one who works with tigers, and that vibe, my friend, is a weird one.

We were like, "Perfect. Let's send him the script so he can read the scene in context, and we'll see what he says."

In the scene, I climb out of a window under the cover of night and crawl into a big open field to retrieve the missile, and that's where I encounter the tiger. We're about a dozen feet apart, staring at each other. Then the tiger charges and I try to run, but it tackles me, just as the missile hits it in the head, killing it.

A few days later, we got a message that Randy had read the script and thought it was no problem whatsoever, which made sense: In the grand scale of tiger shit, this seemed simple. It was supposed to stand there looking at me, roar, then run at me and tackle me (this part would be Randy, in my wardrobe), then it would be replaced by a fake dead tiger.

We were scheduled to shoot the scene in about six weeks, and Randy said he would lose weight to make sure he could fit into my wardrobe and effectively double me in the scene. "I've been looking for an excuse anyway! It's perfect!"

We began shooting, and about a week before the tiger scene, we had a call with Randy to go over all the last-minute details before he drove the tiger from Calgary to Vancouver.

If there was a checklist of things you did NOT want to hear a tiger trainer say, he hit every single item.

ME: Hey, Randy! How's the weight loss going? I hope good! I'm not trying to be in a lot of scenes with this tiger.

RANDY: Oh yeah! It's great. Perfect. I feel great. Alright, I just wanna go over some details.

ME: Alright, cool.

RANDY: So . . . this scene—it's not literally being filmed in a big open field, is it?

ME: Uh . . . yeah. Of course it is.

RANDY: . . . Okay.

ME: Is that bad?

RANDY: It's just a bit harder to contain them in big open areas.

ME: Okay . . . is that a problem?

RANDY: No . . . it should be okay.

ME: . . . Okay. As long as you're sure.

RANDY: I am. As long as there's no chance that, like, a deer or something might be in the area.

ME: Well, we're filming in Squamish, which is in the mountains outside Vancouver, and there's actually a VERY good chance there'll be deer in the area.

RANDY: . . . Okay.

ME: Is that bad?

RANDY: Well, if the tiger sees one, he might run after it, and that might be hard to contain . . . but, you know, as long as there's lights and crew around, I'm sure the deer will stay away. It'll be fine.

ME: You sure?

RANDY: Yep! Completely.

ME: Okay . . .

RANDY: As long as we're not shooting at night.

ME: Well, the scene is set in the middle of the night, and we are filming it at night.

RANDY: Oh . . .

ME: Is that a problem?

RANDY: Well . . . tigers hunt at night.

ME: Okay . . .

RANDY: So . . . you know, they're a lot more aggressive at night.

ME: Well, is that going to be an issue?!

RANDY: . . . You know, it might be good! He'll be more lively, give a better performance.

ME: Are you sure?

RANDY: Yep! Completely! It's fine. This is a good tiger. He'll be great. As long as it's not raining.

ME: Well, it's the Pacific Northwest in February; it'll almost definitely be raining.

Silence.

ME: Is that bad?

RANDY: . . . Well . . . the rain really agitates them.

ME: Should we not do this?

About fifteen seconds of silence.

RANDY: No, it's fine! We'll be fine!

ME: You sure?

RANDY: Yep!

The night the tiger arrived, I was incredibly nervous. I turned to Evan, who was co-directing the film with me, and I was like, "There's no actual reason for me and this tiger to be anywhere near each other. We can just shoot it in halves and combine the shots; you'll never know I wasn't near it."

EVAN: If we have time. We didn't really schedule it that way; it'll take twice as much time to shoot it like that.

ME: I just don't wanna be in the same physical vicinity as the tiger.

EVAN: As long as Randy lost weight and doubles you well, you shouldn't really have to be.

We walked up to the set and saw an animal trailer parked to the side of the giant valley we were shooting in. Then I saw Randy, in my wardrobe, but not a pound smaller than he was before. He looked nothing like me at all. He might have even gained weight.

RANDY: You lost weight!

ME: No I didn't! I've been wearing the same suit for the last five weeks!

RANDY: Well, I guess I was going off of how you used to look, because you lost weight, it seems.

As a side note, people are always treating me like I just lost a ton of weight, even though I've basically been the same weight since 2009, which is kind of nice and also kind of insulting.

ME: Well, I don't think you're gonna be able to double me.

RANDY: Then let's have you meet Frank!

ME: Who's Frank? A thinner tiger trainer?

RANDY: No! He's the tiger! If you're gonna shoot with him, he should start getting used to you!

ME: I don't want to shoot with him or get to know him at all!

RANDY: Then what should we do?

I looked over at Evan, who looked at me like: "Fuck you, go meet the tiger." (This is one of the instances where directing and acting really come in conflict with each other.)

ME: Fine.

I walked over to the trailer with Randy and his sixteen-year-old son, who is also a tiger trainer, as Evan and the rest of the crew stood a few hundred yards away, watching.

The trailer door opened and out walked a tiger. He came right up to me. His head was the diameter of a manhole cover and went up to my chest. It was truly terrifying, and it made me think that anyone who thought that keeping these things in cages was a good idea was a complete weirdo, which made me further question the judgment of Randy, who held my life in his hands at this point, which then made me REALLY question my own judgment, 'cause I was actively trusting my life with this weirdo and his tiger.

Frank nuzzled against me a few times, walking around me in circles. It was astonishing.

RANDY: **He likes you!**

ME: **How can you tell? He's not eating me?**

RANDY: **Exactly!**

ME: **Where did you get this tiger?**

RANDY: **I bought it from a stripper. She had a tiger cub as part of her act, and then she realized it was gonna eat her onstage eventually! Ha!**

ME: **Yeah! Hilarious.**

As we began filming the scene, I realized I would actually have to lie on the ground on my stomach in front of the tiger, which is wayyyyy scarier than standing in front of it; I couldn't have been more vulnerable. The tiger was doing what it was supposed to do, for the most part. At one point we wanted a shot of it roaring, but it wouldn't do anything other than just sit there with a normal tiger face.

RANDY: **I know what to do. Don't tell anyone about this.**

He proceeded to go behind the tiger trailer, piss in his glove, and approach the tiger.

RANDY: **You rolling?**

We were.

He rubbed his pissy glove in the tiger's face, which didn't make it roar but instead open its mouth wide and recoil as if it was saying, "Really, motherfucker? After all this, you're rubbing piss in my fucking face?"

Randy turned back to us, proud. "You can put a roar sound in there in post! It'll look like he's roaring!"

What's annoying is he was right.

I've never been more relieved than I was when I saw Frank get loaded back in his truck, but I honestly felt terrible for the animal. I eventually found an online campaign with the mission of shutting down Randy and his tiger zoo, and I donated a bunch of money to it. Today, Randy and his tiger farm are no longer in operation. I still think of that tiger and hope he's doing okay and that, before they closed the zoo, he took a big bite out of Randy's fat ass.

VERIFICATION

"What would you do if the president told his followers to kill a specific American citizen?" I asked Jack Dorsey, the CEO of Twitter.

Long silence.

JACK: **I'd like to think that would be something that would require some action.**

ME: **You'd like to think?! You haven't talked about it?**

JACK: **Not that specifically.**

ME: **So, you'd like to think it would require some action, but you're not SURE that it would? Maybe you'd just let him tell his followers to kill someone?**

JACK: **Well . . .**

The call was not going well.

I vividly remember my dad telling me at a young age: "People hate Jews." I didn't really believe him. It just didn't make sense. Jews? Us? What's to hate? But, as I got older, I realized that for sure, yes, people hate Jews.

My "friends" in high school would say "wej" as a word for "cheap," which I didn't realize until YEARS LATER was "Jew" spelled backward. We said so many stupid things, and my antenna was so not tuned to anti-Semitism that it didn't even register. It wasn't until I was in my mid-twenties that I was like, *Oh, those guys were all being horrible to us.*

I think one of the reasons people hate Jews is because we pass for non-Jews. We're interlopers. Shhh . . . we could be anywhere. And we might look like white Christians, but we don't believe what they believe, which just freaks the fuck out of people. There's almost an implicit deception at play. People feel tricked by Jews. And people only like being tricked by magicians and wizards, who, not coincidentally, are very likely *visually* based on Jews.

Once I started working in Hollywood, anti-Semitism was more hidden for the most part. There are a lot of Jewish people working in the entertainment industry—an industry that was essentially created by Jewish people, so it adds up—just like there are a lot of Swedish people in the assemble-it-yourself furniture industry.

The first really overt act of aggressive anti-Semitism happened in the last place I would have expected it: an elevator with Eddie Griffin at the opening of the Planet Hollywood Las Vegas Resort & Casino.

It was 2007, and to help celebrate the opening of the new Planet Hollywood, they offered to fly a bunch of famous people to Vegas to essentially go to parties for a few days. Me and Lauren thought it sounded fun, and a few of our other friends said they would go, too.

The first night, we went to a party where I met Sylvester Stallone. Sylvester Stallone is a name that has been in my life for as long as I can remember. He's been famous since I've had any real cognition, and his name never sounded *that* strange to me. But then I met him.

"Hi, I'm Sylvester."

His voice rumbled my loins, like a lion's roar.

"Hi, Sylvester." That's when I realized that there is no other human on earth named Sylvester. There's a cartoon cat named Sylvester, but literally no other human I've ever met. I've been alive almost forty years. I've met a grand total of one Sylvester, and it was Stallone. It's a VERY rare name. And to say the name "Sylvester" out loud to a person named "Sylvester" really makes you realize just how strange a name "Sylvester" is. It's bizarre. For some reason "Sylvester Stallone" isn't that weird. The "Stallone" somehow anchors it in normalcy. But you take that away and find yourself with just "Sylvester" dangling out there like a dick in the breeze, and you understand how odd it is.

If you're thinking, *That's not that weird of a name,* then you're just exposing yourself as someone who's never been face-to-face with a Sylvester. And by that I mean, you're somebody who has never met Sylvester Stallone, because, again, there is only one Sylvester on the planet, and it's him.

This isn't a singular phenomenon. I always thought "Sigourney Weaver" was a pretty normal name, until I met her. The "Weaver" is doing a lot of heavy lifting with that one. It makes the whole name roll off the tongue. But when a tall, beautiful woman comes up to you backstage at Comic-Con and says, "Hi! I'm Sigourney!" it's absolutely shocking.

Later that night, me, Lauren, and Jonah Hill found ourselves waiting for an elevator to go back to our rooms. Because Vegas is a horrible clusterfuck at all times, it was taking forever for an elevator to come, so we were psyched when the doors finally opened. But there was a giant security guard standing there, blocking the entrance.

"Sorry, this one's private."

Then a voice came from behind the guard. "No, wait!"

Eddie Griffin popped out. He eyed us. "Actually, let them in. I wanna ride with them."

I'll take this moment to say there is very little rhyme or reason to which celebrities have security and which ones don't. I've seen some of the biggest stars navigate the world relatively easily with nobody helping or protecting them. I've also seen untalented comedians who nobody really gives a flying fuck about have huge security details, but I won't name names.

Back to Eddie Griffin and his huge security detail.

They allowed us entrance to his elevator, and we hit the button.

EDDIE: I'm glad I saw you guys! I saw your movie! The high school movie!

JONAH: Cool! That's awesome.

EDDIE: Yeah, I've been trying to make a movie for a while now, but nobody will make it. But they made yours, and you know why?

ME: No! Why?

EDDIE: Because I'm Black and you're Jewish motherfuckers!

We kind of all awkwardly laughed, thinking, praying, that this was some sort of terrible joke. You know, the kind Eddie Griffin is famous for. His guards laughed, too.

ME: Oh yeah? What do you mean by that?

EDDIE: I mean, you Jewish motherfuckers run Hollywood and you only make movies with other Jewish motherfuckers!

Ohhhhh, I remember thinking, *this isn't a joke. This dude is just going on a wild anti-Semitic tirade to me, Jonah, and Lauren, while we're trapped in a VERY long elevator ride with him.* His security stopped laughing.

Jonah said, "Uh . . . sorry, I guess?" trying to make a joke.

Shockingly, Eddie was not as in tune with comedy as one might expect from a performer of his caliber, so he didn't get that Jonah was just trying to let him off the hook and move on.

EDDIE: Don't be sorry! Tell your Jews to let other people make some movies!

Bing! We hit his floor and he got off.

We all tried to process how insane it was—not just insane that he would say that to us, but insane because he's really ignoring the fact that if there's one thing that Jewish people are NOT above, it's making money producing things that are fronted by Black people. Anyone who's ever seen a biopic of any Black musician knows the character I'm talking about, and he's usually very appropriately played by my dear friend David Krumholtz.

David Krumholtz in Ray.

Anti-Semitic incidents were few and far between for a while after that, but that all changed when I joined Twitter. I was constantly getting attacked by these stupid white-supremacist assholes, which is annoying, but what really pissed me off was that a lot of them were verified by Twitter.

I realized that Jack Dorsey, the co-founder and CEO of Twitter, followed me, so I started DMing him to express my unhappiness that his platform was verifying accounts that spread this Nazi propaganda. I pointed out that sites like Gab and countless other assholes were using their verified status on Twitter to blatantly promote white supremacy and also intimidate and threaten people who disagreed with them.

They were doxxing enemies and spreading ideas that manifested actual violence. Over DM, Jack just kept saying, "We plan on reworking this. . . . We plan on reworking this."

He didn't seem that concerned or bothered, and as far as I could discern, he didn't seem like he gave a fuck.

And then I tweeted that feeling.

Seth Rogen ✓
@Sethrogen

I've been DMing with @jack about his bizarre need to verify white supremacists on his platform for the last 8 months or so, and after all the exchanges, I've reached a conclusion: the dude simply does not seem to give a fuck.

8:28 AM · Jul 3, 2018 · Twitter for iPhone

34.1K Retweets **2.9K** Quote Tweets **153.7K** Likes

Jack wasn't thrilled with me (although the white supremacy itself didn't seem to bug him) and he reached out to get on the phone. I can only assume he hoped I would feel better about the situation after our talk.

I felt catastrophically worse.

I asked him to explain how the verification process works. He said that it basically started as something he would give to his friends. A token he'd hand out to the cool kids, and by cool, I mean people who are friends with Jack Dorsey.

The next evolution of verification on Twitter came after a natural disaster, in an attempt to prevent the flow of false information and fraudulent charities. He actually did something good! Some government bodies started to be verified, as well. Then, through a series of events that Jack himself can't explain with any certainty, verification is where it is— a place that makes no fucking sense.

One would probably assume that verification is just a way of making sure you are who you say you are. But one would be wrong, because Twitter has *de*-verified some people, not for being exposed as impostors but because their tweets have been deemed unsavory. So . . . it's not really a verification; it's an endorsement.

Also, you might be very logically thinking, *What's the big deal about being verified? It's just a blue check,* which is what I thought—before I found out that being verified DOES prioritize and push your tweets across the platform. If you're verified, Twitter will amplify your message.

I tried desperately to understand Jack's take on the situation.

I started with the elephant in the room.

ME (TRYING TO SOUND SMART): You're aware that, almost weekly, the president is in blatant violation of your terms of service with regard to abusive behavior, threats, and harassment, and that kinda tells everyone that you don't care about your own terms of service. It seems like you're choosing what to enforce and not enforce, and right now you're not enforcing very much regarding white supremacy.

JACK: Yeah. I really hear that. We have to rework the verification process from the ground up.

ME: When do you plan on doing that?

JACK: Umm ... yeah ... We don't know right now. First and foremost, I think our communication is failing us.

ME: I kinda think what you're communicating is failing you.

JACK: Well, first and foremost, we're dedicated to promoting healthy conversation.

ME: Huh? What?

JACK: Healthy conversation. A healthy dialogue. Conversation ...

ME: How do you promote healthy conversation?

JACK: We're working on that.

ME: Okay ... well, in the meantime, do you plan on de-verifying some white supremacists? Just so their message isn't amplified? I'd imagine it's easy to monitor their tweets to see if they're abusive or harmful.

JACK: We don't have the resources to do this.

ME: Huh?

JACK: We really just don't have the resources to do that at this time.

ME (TRYING NOT TO CONDESCEND TO A GUY WHO CREATED A BILLION-DOLLAR COMPANY): Uh ... well, I run a small company, and even I know that "I don't have enough employees to make sure my highly profitable platform is operating in a way that won't get people murdered and Nazis won't come into power" is not a great excuse. I mean ... how about you hire more people? Like a "No Nazis" group?

JACK: We're looking into that.

ME: I mean, this isn't some nebulous, abstract problem. Honestly, in less time than it's taking for you to talk to me, you could just ban or at least de-verify, like, fifteen dangerous white-supremacist accounts. That could save people's lives. I'll tell you who they are right now while we're on the phone!

JACK: **But remember, Seth . . .**

I awaited his amazing founder wisdom.

JACK: **Twitter is merely a mirror of society.**

This drove me nuts. Like Twitter is some beautiful child that Jack had birthed into the world, squozen from his loins, an autonomous creature whose will is to be respected and revered, wherever it should take us.

ME: **You might want to think that, but, like any creation, Twitter is an expression and representation of its creator. There's a reason that people don't hate Instagram. I've met the guy who created it. He's lovely. So, Twitter is a mirror of you. When people are saying Twitter is a cesspool—that's you.**

The call ended badly.

About a month later, I noticed yet another barrage of anti-Semitic tweets from some verified accounts.

Ron Paul tweeted a violently anti-Semitic cartoon, and a verified user named "Roosh" was spreading the idea that all mass shootings were perpetrated by Jews. Another user was offering to pay the legal fees of anyone who assaulted me, which I can only assume he got from Trump, who's said the same shit about people who assault his protesters. Jack got back to me and said he'd "look into it." For some crazy reason, I actually believed him.

A few weeks later, in October 2018, I found myself living in downtown Pittsburgh. I had just moved there for a few months to film *An American Pickle*. I woke up one Saturday morning and checked my phone, learning about the Tree of Life terrorist attack minutes after it started, about three miles from where I was sitting. It would go on to be the worst act of anti-Jewish violence in the history of the United States of America. I felt sick to my stomach. I spent the day walking around the city. Everywhere I went, I saw the same shocked look on people's faces.

People were asking, "How could this happen?" And unfortunately, the answer is obvious. First, it's real easy to get your hands on a high-powered assault rifle in America. Combine that with a president who de-stigmatized outward hatred and social-media platforms that allow people to stoke flames of hatred to the point of combustion.

Because of Twitter, the shooter didn't see himself as a villain. He saw himself as a hero. This guy thought Jews were facilitating the entrance of terrorists into the country—an idea that's perpetuated by countless verified Twitter accounts, right-wing news outlets, and GOP politicians. And without Jack doing anything to stop the spread of these lies, all he was telling people was that they were NOT lies. If they were, he wouldn't be endorsing and amplifying them, right? Wouldn't he take the verification away from the people who spread these lies if they *were* in fact lies? No action, no infraction. It all must be true.

One of the first times the militant and anti-Semitic right wing started to target me online was after I told off Ben Carson for saying that Jews could have protected themselves better during the Holocaust if they'd had easier access to guns. A crazy idea that not only blames Jews for being victims but uses the deaths of the Holocaust to bolster America's ridiculous gun laws.

These victim-blaming talking points were being repeated just hours after the shooting, not only by the media but by the president himself. The idea that it's up to the threatened classes to protect themselves from bigots rather than up to the bigots not to spread hatred and act on their terrible instincts is as stupid as, well, Trump.

"Everyone knows people hate Jews! Lock the doors next time!"

So comforting.

Jack's "too little, too late" approach to monitoring his own website really kicked into high gear around the 2020 presidential election.

After losing the election, Trump did something nobody, except those with eyes and a brain, saw coming. He refused to admit he lost. And the spineless fuckheads in the GOP decided to support this lie, even though they knew it was complete bullshit. Lucky for them, their supporters don't care about reality, so it was ultimately an easy lie to sell.

In the days following the election, Jack took action that he probably thought was super-helpful: Every time Trump tweeted a lie about election fraud, he put a little notice under the tweet saying that some news sources disputed the information in the tweet. Keep in mind, at this same time, verified "news" sites like One America News Network (OANN) and Newsmax were also supporting Trump's Twitter lies, effectively negating whatever these little notices were supposed to be doing in the first place.

Twitter allowed Trump and other verified feeds to spread the lie that the election was stolen until there was a violent and deadly insurrection on January 6, 2021, the day the electoral college votes were being officially counted.

After that, I guess Jack scrounged up some more resources, because he finally banned Trump from Twitter, and the following week, misinformation about the election dropped 75 percent.

As of the writing of this, OANN, Newsmax, and dozens of politicians and "journalists" are still verified by Twitter despite pushing the dangerous lie that there was mass voter fraud in the 2020 election and that Trump actually won, even though there's absolutely no evidence to support this.

Gab, the white-supremacist social-media site, is still verified and having its message amplified by Twitter. Roosh, the verified user I pointed out to Jack years ago, is still verified, and as of this writing, Twitter is amplifying his messages that the Jews committed the Tree of Life shooting *themselves* to curry political favor.

Acts of anti-Semitism went up 57 percent in 2019.

(You can follow me on Twitter @sethrogen.)

XENU

I get as awkward and uncomfortable around famous people as any person who is not famous. If anything, I might get more awkward, because I'm a HUGE movie fan. I love them so much I dedicated my entire life to them, so I get starstruck.

What being famous affords you is a high level of access. And not only are you meeting these famous people, which again, is strange in the first place, but you're meeting them in incredibly odd situations.

I've been in a ton of elevators with famous people, which, as I've illustrated, can be terrible. You generally acknowledge that you are, indeed, both famous people, and some level of conversation is expected. I felt so bad for Bono the time he desperately tried to converse with me in a long freight-elevator ride at 30 Rock.

The most awkward elevator ride I ever went on was at the Oscars. I was about to present an award and found myself in an elevator with Heath Ledger's parents, about thirty seconds after they had just accepted his posthumous Oscar for *The Dark Knight*. I stared at them silently and awkwardly as they stood there, holding the statue. I felt like I had to say something, and to this day I regret my choice:

"Congratulations!"

But short interactions are manageable. It's the long exposure that becomes tricky. Trying to relate to megastars for substantial amounts of time is grueling, if not impossible. And never was that more clear than the time we were beckoned to Tom Cruise's house.

It was 2006, and we were in the middle of filming the movie *Knocked Up*, and Tom Cruise was in the middle of having what seemed like a manic episode in the most public way imaginable. He was dating Katie Holmes, leaping off furniture at the mere thought of his feelings for her. They had just had a baby, Suri, but no image of the child had been published, leading to genuine speculation as to whether or not she even existed. The fact that the thought, *Hey, I wonder if he is just pretending to have a baby,* was even on the table speaks to how strangely the public viewed him at that time.

And in the midst of all that, Judd comes up to me on set one day.

JUDD: **Tom Cruise wants to meet us!**

ME: **What? Why?**

JUDD: **He's thinking of doing a comedy and wants to brainstorm.**

ME: **And we want to take this meeting?**

JUDD: **Of course! We're going as soon as we wrap filming for the day.**

When we finished shooting, I drove across town toward

Tom's house, which was right above Sunset Boulevard. I was nervous for a lot of reasons.

I wasn't sure we should be meeting with him at all. He seemed to be in a strange place, and the idea of becoming the outlet for a manic movie star's desire to publicly restore his image was a service I wanted to reserve for myself. I also just generally didn't like meeting really famous people, because it gave me anxiety and I almost always felt worse after I met them.

I was running late, and I had to pee very, very badly. As I drove up Sunset, I couldn't find anywhere to go, and I started to get worried that the first words I'd speak to Tom Cruise would be, "I'm about to pee in my pants. Can I please use your restroom?!"

I pulled up to the gate and hit the buzzer. "I'm here to see Tom!"

The gate SLOWLY opened. I was actually going to pee in my pants, which would be the worst impression one could make. I started to snake up his long, wooded driveway, when I noticed a Snapple bottle on the floor of my car. I had no choice. I stopped halfway up the driveway and peed into the Snapple bottle. It came dangerously close to overflowing. I sealed the lid, put the bottle in my back seat, and continued up the driveway. After a turn around a bend, I arrived at a huge house with Tom Cruise, Katie Holmes, and little baby Suri waiting to greet me.

I gave him a hearty handshake, which I still feel guilty about given the circumstances.

I had actually met Katie before, because I was in an episode of *Dawson's Creek* a few years earlier. She had a vague "please rescue me from this place" look on her face. The baby was adorable—and real.

Judd arrived a couple minutes later, and we went to Tom's screening room to sit down and chat. We talked for about five hours, and it was a ride. We talked about movies we loved, what we were making, things like that. He told some stories about Stanley Kubrick, which were great to hear, and talked about this new director, J. J. Abrams, whom he was working with on the new *Mission: Impossible* movie.

It was all totally normal . . . until . . . it wasn't.

For those of you who don't know, Scientology is a religion/cult/pyramid scheme invented by coke-addled/moron/science-fiction writer L. Ron Hubbard. Basically, Scientologists believe that seventy-five million years ago, there was a "Galactic Confederacy" that was ruled by an evil alien named Xenu. Xenu brought billions of his alien friends to earth, put them in a volcano, and exploded them with a hydrogen bomb. The spirits of the aliens, known as Thetans, adhered to the spirits of humans on earth, and the journey of becoming a high-ranking Scientologist is one of shedding your Thetans and becoming "clear" of them. Then you get superpowers and shit. Overall, it's not much crazier than any other religion, but the fact that it was literally made by a guy who wrote terrible science-fiction books that essentially have the same plot probably docks it a few points. Also, they don't believe in treating mental illness or depression with drugs.

About four hours into the meeting, it finally came up: The conversation slowwwwwwwly veered into how the public thought he was . . . losing his mind.

Tom: **Well, yeah, they're making it seem like I'm losing my mind.**

Judd: **Making it seem like it?**

Tom: **Yeah. There's a coordinated effort to make it appear that way.**

ME: Who would do that?

TOM: The pharmaceutical industry.

ME: . . . Oh yeah?

TOM: Yeah!

JUDD: . . . And why would they do that?

TOM: Because my exposure of their fraud has cost them SO much money that they're desperate. They're scrambling and they're doing everything they can to discredit me so I won't hurt sales anymore.

ME: Big Pharma made you jump on Oprah's couch?

TOM: They edited it to make it look so much worse than it was. They do that all the time. You should see what they do to my friend Louis Farrakhan!

Of all the strange sentences I've heard in my life, this one coming out of Tom Cruise's mouth is in the top three.

JUDD: Well, Farrakhan has said a lot of blatantly anti-Semitic things.

TOM: No! He's great!

JUDD: He's great? He's compared Jews to cockroaches.

TOM: No! See, that's the media! They're distorting all of it! Take my religion, for example—Scientology. They make it seem sooooo fucking different than it is! If you just gave me like an hour to tell you about it, you'd be like, "No fucking way?! That's what Scientology is?! No fucking way!!" In just one hour, I could completely change your minds!

Me and Judd looked at each other. Do we bite? Are we strong enough to be proselytized to by one of the most famous and charismatic men on the planet? Would I come out of this thinking I had to expunge alien spirits from my soul?

JUDD: Yeah . . . maybe another time.

We left soon after that, and I was driving back down his long, now-dark driveway. I had passed the spot where I'd stopped to pee in the bottle, when I saw it: a red light coming from the trees. I squinted. . . . It was a video camera, with its little red recording light now visible, pointing directly where I had peed. If a camera could wink, this one would have.

Am I kept up at night by the thought that Tom Cruise likely has video footage of me urinating in a Snapple bottle in my car? No. But if I ever start expounding on the virtues of clearing one's Thetans, you know it's bad and he's blackmailing me.

The next day at work, Judd had all these ideas for Tom. I remember I was like, "He's not just meeting with us! He looks crazy and he's just trying to be in a comedy so he seems in on the joke! We can't be the only ones he's talking to about this."

JUDD: **Maybe, but I think we can get him. . . .**

A few months later, he signed on to be in *Tropic Thunder*. He was hilarious and everyone loved him again the second they saw it.

ACID

was always afraid to do acid, but, dear god, I wanted to. I think the propaganda got to me. I remember hearing as a kid that if you did acid once, you could get "acid flash-backs" for life. That at any moment you could suddenly find yourself in the throes of hallucinogenic hysteria. I remember a kid in school telling me that if you EVER did acid, you couldn't be an airplane pilot, just in case a flashback happened mid-flight.

I also heard stories about bad trips—people thinking they could fly and jumping out of windows, people thinking there were spiders crawling all over them and tearing their skin off . . . genuinely horrifying shit to think about confronting, especially when coupled with the fact that the OTHER thing I'd always heard about acid was how long it lasted: over twelve hours sometimes.

It had kind of a "cult-y" connotation, too, so that made it scary. I remember hearing that Charles Manson drugged his followers with acid so they'd become murdering, brain-washed zombies, which isn't the greatest commercial for a drug. I also watched the *Woodstock* documentary, which captures the moment a man stands in front of the crowd specifically to warn everyone that there's some bad brown acid going around and to stay the fuck away from it.

Sure, I'd heard about "seeing the music, tasting the colors," and that stuff, but still, throughout high school and the years after, me and my friends steered clear, instead opting for herculean amounts of shrooms.

Shrooms had taken me on some pretty intense trips over the years, and the thought that acid was *more* intense made it downright terrifying to even consider. But there was always one voice in my head that stuck out. The voice of a guy at summer camp, who was like, "Acid is wayyyy less intense than shrooms!"

"Really?"

"Yeah. With shrooms, you're the passenger. With acid, you're the *driver.*"

Well, I could definitely attest to the first part, but I straight up didn't believe the second part.

As I got older, I got more curious. And I found myself around people who were on acid from time to time, and they didn't seem like they'd jump out a window or tear their skin off. They actually seemed coherent and like they were having a great fucking time. So, because I'm wildly on the nose, at the age of thirty-six, me and some other friends who had never done acid all booked a place in Joshua Tree to try it for the first time.

My friend Ben flew in from Vancouver, and we planned to arrive on Friday morning, get the place ready, and then Kyle,

Ariel, and Evan would come in the afternoon. We'd take the acid at around 4 P.M. and then . . . see what happened?

We got to the Yucca Valley, where there's a giant military base and a fuck-ton of barbershops and very sketchy-looking massage parlors, giving the impression that this town had a lot of well-groomed servicemen who loved themselves a good hand job. Which is good, I guess. I want our armed forces to be clean-cut and not in any way sexually pent-up.

We found a health-food store and bought whatever we could find that seemed tasty. We weren't really sure what we'd want to eat; drugs and food mix differently depending on what you're on. On most drugs, you can just avoid eating altogether, but acid lasts so fucking long that we were gonna have to eat eventually.

We were anxious about doing the acid, as doing any new drug is scary. I was particularly nervous because, a few weeks earlier, at Martin's place, I had a wild fucking time on shrooms and was still a bit shell-shocked.

My friend Martin had just moved into a new house with a pool, and me, Evan, and our friend Andrew made a plan to go to Martin's, eat a bit of shroom chocolate, get a tour of the new house, and then go hang out by the pool as the shrooms kicked in and just overall have a chill night.

We got to Martin's and he had rose-shaped shroom chocolates waiting for us.

MARTIN: There's gold caps in here!

ME: How much?

MARTIN: Not sure exactly . . .

We each ate a chocolate and began the tour. As we were admiring the sconces in the guest room, we all looked at each other.

ME: Are you guys REALLY starting to feel this shit?

EVAN: I'm very much starting to feel it.

MARTIN: This shit is coming on hard and fast as a mother-fucker . . . whooooooooooooo.

We couldn't even finish one lap of the house. I went down to the dining room and held on to the table for dear life. My hands melted into the wood up to the wrist, and the swirly pattern of the grain started to work its way up my arms. No matter how many times I shook my head, the hallucination stuck.

ME: Hoooolllllyyyy fuuuuuuuck!!!!

Andrew appeared holding a sword, which is never a good thing while on shrooms.

ANDREW: Look at the size of this letter opener!

I laughed hysterically till I wept. I looked at the time. It had only been twenty minutes since we had eaten the chocolate. This was just starting and was going to get steadily more intense for the next few hours. Good lord, I was in for it.

My brain then felt like it was ripped out of my head and thrown into a kaleidoscope. I struggled to operate doors, light switches, faucets—simple things I've had a pretty good handle on for quite some time. I lay on a lawn chair for hours, weeping about how much I missed seeing my wife and my dog due to my work schedule, and the next day I quit two jobs because I had the cosmic revelation that they weren't great uses of my time.

When you're so high you're calling your employer the next day to quit your job, you know you've done a lot of drugs.

Me and Ben drove from the grocery store to the house we rented, near the outskirts of Joshua Tree National Park. When we got there, it kind of reminded me of where Sarah

Connor's friends live in *Terminator 2*, the place with the underground bunker where Arnold gets the minigun. It had a bit of a "survivalist" vibe. But it also had an outdoor fireplace, so we were psyched.

The others arrived and Evan pulled out the acid. It was on little tiny paper tabs, which surprised me for some reason. We each took a tab and put it on our tongue. It was one of those moments when I thought, *I've only ever seen this in movies, and it always looked exactly like this*. Which is also what I'll probably think when a tsunami wipes out Los Angeles.

I was scared shitless. My heart was pounding. I strapped myself in . . . and was pleasantly surprised.

It came on a bit weird, with a kind of chemical-y feeling, but around an hour and a half after we took it, we were fully in the throes, and it was wonderful. It was way less intense than shrooms—at least the amount I had been taking—and although I was decidedly fucked off my ass, I did in fact feel like I was in the driver's seat. For the most part . . .

The time came to eat. We were starving, which again, was kind of a surprise.

We all went to the kitchen and laid out what we had gotten at the health-food store:

Tortillas
Chicken breast
Potatoes
Feta cheese

KYLE: **What the fuck is this?**
BEN: **Mmmm . . . I'm not sure.**
EVAN: **What did you plan on making?**
BEN: **Well, I'm not sure! We didn't really talk about it.**

ARIEL: Why not?

ME: We've been fucking stressed out all day about doing this fucking acid!

BEN: The nerves got to us!

ME: We weren't thinking right!

ARIEL: No shit. These groceries don't make sense! There's no meal you can make with this!

BEN: Sure there is!

KYLE: What? It's like some fucked-up Top Chef challenge! Do acid and make a meal with a bunch of ingredients that don't make sense. We're gonna starve to death!

BEN: No! Shut up! I got this! We're having fucking Greek chicken tortillas with mashed potatoes! Don't worry! I got this . . .

As we sat in the living room, we could hear Ben working hard around the corner. After about twenty minutes he yelled, "Guys, this is going to be fucking GROSS!"

After dinner, even though there was room for each of us to have our own bedroom, we all gathered in a little bunk room together. It felt like camp, except every time I closed my eyes, I saw spider legs appear and peel away layers of reality, but in a not-at-all-scary way. Whenever it got unpleasant I could steer it away, because, again, with acid it felt like I was in the driver's seat. With shrooms, at best I'm in the passenger seat, but more often I'm strapped to the hood, holding on for dear life.

My first experience was great, and I did the perfect amount. But there was this nagging thought in my head. It's not a great thought but one that I stand by: You haven't really done a drug till you've done a bit too much of it.

Luckily, the next year, at Burning Man, I did too much acid.

If you don't know, Burning Man is essentially a giant art festival. To get there, you drive an RV to the middle of fucking nowhere in the Nevada desert and then turn off the only road and go two hours farther into what's REALLY the middle of fucking nowhere. They sell nothing and have nothing other than porta-potties—no plumbing, no garbage cans, no stores, no water. You bring everything you need, and you dispose of everything you use in your own camp and take it all with you when you leave. They call it "radical self-reliance," but it's mostly just eating a ton of microwavable burritos for three days straight.

I completely get why people are annoyed by the concept of it, and before I went, I was, too. But ultimately it's a drug wonderland, so it won me over. Whatever Disneyland is for kids who like cartoons is what Burning Man is to adults who like hallucinogens. Mostly you ride bikes around the moonlike landscape, high off your fucking ass, going from one giant art installation to the next, which is pretty much the most fun thing one can do.

About fifteen of our friends made a camp on the outskirts of the festival, and as the sun was setting, I took two hits of acid. About twenty minutes later, it came on fast. My first trip was a beautiful if not tiny-bit-rocky metamorphosis from sober to high; this felt more like a scene in a movie where someone turns into a werewolf. I wanted to tear my clothes off. I had to remind myself to breathe. The thought of engaging in any sort of conversation was appalling. As my friends congregated to go out for the night, I stood alone, looking out into the desert, thinking, *What the fuck did I just do to myself?!*

But about five minutes later . . . I was just really high. I thought, *As long as I don't have to navigate any* actual *high-*

stakes situations that require my brain or common sense or anything, I'll be fine!

Unfortunately, Burning Man does have actual high-stakes situations that require your brain and common sense, because, well, they burn shit. It's actually the worst part about Burning Man to me, which makes it confusing in that it's their titular selling point. It'd be like if an art gallery was bragging about the fact that they were gonna destroy all the art after the exhibition was over. It's a strange stance. Even stranger is the feeling that some of this shit was made just to be burned, which is maybe poetic to some people but not to me. A festival brought to you by the weirdo you hung out with as a kid who poured lighter fluid on all his toys and melted them? Fantastic!

Lauren and me were still high on acid—her, the perfect amount, and me, still a bit too much but stabilizing. We were watching a giant four-story structure be burned to the ground, when suddenly the wind shifted and giant pieces of flaming debris started to rain down on the area we were in. People scrambled for cover, but the fire kept falling. Flaming whirlwinds whipped through the crowd; it was pandemonium.

We spotted some cop SUVs parked a few hundred yards away and ran behind them, trying to take cover. The cops were afraid to damage their cruisers, I guess, so they hopped in and drove away from the scene, leaving us exposed again.

As we held hands and ran as fast and far as we could into the desert to escape the flaming wood pieces that were falling all around us, one thought kept rolling through my mind: *Thank fucking god I'm not on shrooms right now.*

All this likely begs the questions: "What's wrong with you, Seth? Why do you do so many drugs and why can't you stop talking about it?" And the best answer to that I can come up with is "They give me insights into my own thinking, feeling, and behavior in ways that I haven't found elsewhere, and they're super-fun." It's really nothing new. People have been getting fucked up for thousands of years. There's something about removing myself from my normal baseline of operation that feels exciting and adventurous. And shared adventures can be incredibly bonding. I think I also keep yapping about drugs like acid, MDMA, and shrooms because of how incredibly fucking bothered I am that they're viewed as these big bad wolves compared to alcohol, which is both way more prevalent and way more shitty for you.

Like, if I told you there was a drug that you drank and it made you have fun for like an hour, then it made you dizzy for three hours, then you blacked out, then the entire next day you had a terrible headache and generally felt like shit, you probably wouldn't be clamoring to try it. But alcohol is so mainstream that it's somehow overcome the fact that it sucks, which is also how I hope to be described one day. But in all seriousness, if I have two glasses of wine, I feel like shit the next day. And the sugar and carbs are objectively bad for your health. I've done so much acid that the desert itself crashed like waves on a beach; it has no sugar, no carbs. In fact, the next day, I felt fucking fantastic.

WOZ AND THE
MAGIC CASTLE

I'd acted in a lot of movies, but I had not played a real person before. Then, in 2015, I got cast to play Steve Wozniak in the film *Steve Jobs*.

I was worried about meeting him at first. I didn't want him to be bummed out that I was playing him. Everyone else had such better actors portraying them. Michael Fassbender, Kate Winslet! Woz got me.

Luckily, he seemed happy with the casting, and meeting him was a true trip. He was the first *inventor* I'd ever met. And he didn't invent just anything. He invented the personal computer. And to make this paragraph truly repetitive, I'll go on to say he didn't just *invent* the personal computer. He CONCEIVED of it.

When Woz was a kid, computers were roughly the size of an elephant and cost about a million dollars, so the idea of owning one was ... far-fetched. It would kind of be like wanting a locomotive—as in, not something anyone could imagine a private citizen owning. Computers were for NASA, not teenagers.

But he wanted one. So badly that he created one. His brilliant mind was able to take circuit boards that were a couple of feet across and rewire them with such artful efficiency that you could hold them in the palm of your hand. His desire to own a computer is the reason we all have one today.

One of the real revelations I had after meeting him was that he was one of the first famous "nerds." And as someone who grew up watching *Revenge of the Nerds* and its sequel *Nerds in Paradise* more than I should have, it was a shocking revelation. Almost every impression of a nerd that you saw in the eighties was kind of based on him. And it made him instantly familiar and kind of nostalgic feeling.

He was friends with the first hackers, and he knew how to use whistles to trick the phone company into letting him make free long-distance calls. He even prank-called the pope once. Woz also has prosopagnosia, otherwise known as "face blindness," which is a condition that doesn't let you remember people's faces, which is also hilarious. He makes it very clear he has this every time you see him, because he doesn't want to seem rude if you've met and he doesn't instantly recognize you. "Hi! Have we met? I don't remember faces!"

Woz loves music, and in the eighties he created the modern music festival: The "US Festival" was the first one with good sound no matter where in the massive venue you were, the first to have giant screens to see the acts, even if you were in the back row. It was even the first to have widely available bathrooms and running water. So next time you're at Coachella, thank Woz. (Also, why would you go to Coachella?)

He booked amazing acts: Talking Heads, the Police, Tom Petty, the Grateful Dead, and more. It drew a crowd of over

425,000 people. He spent 12.5 million dollars of his own money to put the festival on, and after all was said and done, he lost 10 million dollars on it.

"It was a math error!" he told me.

So, what did he do? He doubled down, and the following year he put on another festival, which was twice as big as the first. Held on Memorial Day weekend in 1983, the next US Festival brought in acts like David Bowie, U2, Van Halen, and the Clash.

It turns out whatever mathematical snafu happened the first time happened again, and overall he lost more than 20 million dollars. But Woz didn't give a fuck. "It was so fun! I met David Lee Roth!"

Ironically, much like a lot of Apple computers themselves, Woz's skill set became kind of obsolete not long after it had become revolutionary. Technology caught up with him. The world no longer needed the ability to turn giant circuit boards into tiny ones. He had done it. They were small now.

✿ ✿ ✿

The film we were making explored the relationship between Woz and Jobs, among other things. One of its main ideas was technical abilities versus salesmanship and branding. Jobs was one of the greatest salesmen of all time, and he happened to be friends with the guy who made one of the most important inventions of all time. That was the magic. A technical genius was close with a marketing genius. But the marketing genius, not shockingly, took the spotlight, the acclaim, and a lot of the money. I had no idea that Jobs himself had literally no technical skills when it came to computers. I assumed he had done *something*.

Woz: Nope! He didn't know how to do any of that! That wasn't his thing.

I would always prod Woz about any resentment or jealousy he might have had. He wouldn't budge. "I loved Steve."

Finally, after hours of pestering him one day, I got a story.

Years after Woz left Apple, in the late eighties, he invented the first universal remote control for televisions. He wanted to make a plastic mold for the prototype. Steve Jobs had a guy who made the plastic-mold prototypes for all his Apple products. Woz had gotten to know this guy and knew he was the best there was; otherwise, Steve wouldn't like him so much.

He dropped off the specs, but a few days later got a call from the mold guy.

Mold Guy: I can't do it.

Woz: What? Why not?

Mold Guy: Steve came in and saw your prototype on the shelf and asked what it was, and I told him it was your remote . . . and he said that I couldn't do both. I had to either do his stuff or your stuff . . . so I have to do his stuff.

Woz basically told me that this personal slight upset him

more than the fact that the average person had no sense of his real contribution to society as we know it.

Woz: I never got why he did that. That really bothered me. I mean, I found another guy to do the remote mold, and it was fine, but still . . .

A few months after the movie had wrapped, I was back in L.A. and got an email from Woz. He and his wife wanted to hang out with Lauren and me. They invited us to the Magic Castle. I was thrilled but a little nervous—the last time I had been to the Magic Castle was a complete disaster. And before you start asking, "What the fuck is the Magic Castle?" don't worry. I got you.

The Magic Castle is a social club for magicians that was built into the side of the Hollywood Hills. The building itself is a bit of a magic trick, in that from the outside it looks like a small chalet, but once you get inside, it's a massive social space with bars, theaters, and a steakhouse. Getting inside can be . . . tricky? (Feel free to burn this book now.) You actually need to be invited by a member, and in order to be a member, you have to be a magician.

I had been a few times with small groups, but the year before the Woz invite, I had taken a bunch of people I work with for a night of magic and narcotics. We all took MDMA, and it hit my friend James really hard. He looked like a sweaty disaster and could barely follow a conversation. We got in the front door and stood in line for the close-up magic theater, which holds about thirty people. This shit was no joke. I turned to James.

Me: Hey! James, you okay?

James: Hmm? What? Yeah?

Me: Are you okay?!

James: Yeah. Cool. I'm fine.

ME: Look, if anyone asks you if you want to volunteer or be part of the show in any way, shape, or form, say no.

JAMES: Why?

ME: Because you're fucked, man! You just can't do it! You gotta lay low.

JAMES: Okay, cool. No problem.

A waitress walked up to us.

WAITRESS: Hey, the close-up magic show is about to start. Any of you want to volunteer to be part of the show?

JAMES: I'd love to!

And they took him away. Evan came over.

EVAN: Where are they taking him?

ME: He volunteered!

EVAN: For what?!

ME: To be part of the fucking show.

EVAN: Whoooooooo. Man. I'm FUCKED right now. And I have a way higher tolerance than James, so he must be SUPER-fucked right now!

ME: He is!

EVAN: Fuck!

The waitress returned. "We're ready to seat you for the show!"

We all filed into the small theater. On the stage was a table and a chair. In the chair was James, rolling his fucking face off, smiling ear to ear. We took our seats.

EVAN: This is going to be a disaster.

The magician came out and could instantly see that James was fucked up. But he was in his sixties and very seasoned-looking, so he gave James a look like, "I'm a pro, I've done this for decades. I've seen fucked-up people before, and I can handle them! It's part of the fun! Let's do this!"

MAGICIAN: Pick a card.

JAMES: From where?

MAGICIAN: From this deck.

JAMES: Where in the deck?

MAGICIAN: Anywhere in the deck.

JAMES: I'm not sure which one to pick.

He gave James a card.

MAGICIAN: It's fine. Here's your card. Remember this card.

JAMES: What?

MAGICIAN: Remember the card.

JAMES: What card?

MAGICIAN: This card. The one in your hand?

JAMES: This one? The two of hearts? Remember that?

MAGICIAN: Yes, but don't TELL me the card! Pick another card.

JAMES: What do I do with this card?

MAGICIAN: Put it back.

JAMES: Am I supposed to remember it?

MAGICIAN: No!

JAMES: Okay, 'cause I don't.

MAGICIAN: . . . Wow.

In real time, we were able to watch this seasoned performer discover that he had in fact been doing magic a long time. So long there were NEW drugs that he had never encountered before. Drugs that his old techniques wouldn't work on. Drugs that might render the very concept of magic obsolete. After all, what fun is sleight of hand when you can barely see or understand what the fuck is going on, anyway? A potato chip is impressive when you're on great drugs. Magic is just a lot of effort and deception.

The show ended with a long trick that James ruined by accidentally showing the card to the magician. We left immediately after, and I was worried I'd never be welcomed back. So, when me and Lauren and Woz and his wife, Janet, showed up and were welcomed in with no objections from the management, I was psyched.

I knew Woz was pretty famous, but to magicians, Woz is a king. Magicians are huge nerds, and Woz is literally nerd patient zero. He was bombarded by fans asking for autographs from the second we walked into the club. And he would oblige by taking out and signing uncut sheets of counterfeit American two-dollar bills that a friend of his had printed, because, again, nerds. He watched the magic with awe and delight, audibly exclaiming during every trick. "Ahh!! Whaaa! Haaa!"

After about five and a half hours of watching magic shows with the Wozniaks, we headed out of the club toward the valet. We handed our stub to the attendant, but the Wozniaks just kept walking toward the dark parking lot.

ME: You guys didn't valet?

WOZ: No. Actually, we Segwayed.

LAUREN: You what?

WOZ: Segwayed! We're staying at the W hotel a few miles up Hollywood Boulevard, so we just Segwayed here. Wanna see?

ME: Uh . . . yeah?

They led us across the parking lot to a corner where, propped up against a little shed, were two old Segways.

ME: Bet you got on the Segway bandwagon pretty early?

WOZ: Oh, you bet! These are the first Segways! See?!

He showed me the serial numbers on the handlebars: 001 and 002.

ME: Wow! The first two Segways!

WOZ: Yeah! The only thing is, they didn't create any sort of headlight till later models, so we have to use these.

He pulled two flashlights out of his jacket pocket and gave one to his wife. With one hand operating the Segway, the other holding a flashlight, they drove off, looking as silly and happy as two people could.

Steve Jobs might have gotten more money, recognition, and a better actor to play him, but still, Woz came out on top.

JEWISH SUMMER CAMP

I f you've ever met a Jewish person, there's a good chance you've heard them talk about Jewish summer camp. If you've never met a Jewish person, I recommend it. They're great, and they don't make bread out of baby's blood, unless the baby has EXTRA-tasty blood.

Jewish summer camp is somewhat mystifying, mostly because of the degree to which Jews just fucking love it. The fact that the combination of the terms "Jews" and "camps" hasn't diminished our enthusiasm is a real testament to how psyched on the whole notion we are.

I think there are a few reasons for the popularity. One is that a lot of Jews love nothing more than the idea of making more Jews and nothing less than the idea of there being fewer Jews. And since Jews don't proselytize—largely because I imagine the idea of being a missionary is a big turn-off to Jews, who are notoriously finicky travelers—their best shot of keeping their numbers at an acceptable level is by having their kids impregnate/be impregnated by other Jews and birth little Jews, or "Jeems," as we call them. (This is not true.) And a VERY good place to plant the seeds for this is Jewish camp.

I know what you're thinking: *That's fucking gross. Sending your kids to camp with any thought toward them fucking is super-duper weird.* And I would say in return, "Yes. It is pretty fucking gross, and super-duper weird, and what's even weirder is that these people aren't even that religious, so why are they so invested in Jewish demographics? I don't know. It makes no sense. Jews are strange."

But it doesn't matter. You still feel at peace around the other Jews. I think of my friend who lives in L.A. with corgis, which are those funny short-legged dogs. She read about a corgi farm, where you can take your corgi to herd sheep. Since her dog had lived its whole life in Hollywood, she assumed it would stare at the sheep and maybe brag to them about how efficient the route it took to the farm was. But to her amazement, her corgi instantly started herding, as if just *being* in this environment tapped into some primal instinct. Which is also what it's like being Jewish. Whether you like it or not, it's in you. It shows up on DNA tests. They can find a severed finger and determine if it was once attached to a Jewish hand. It's not like other religions in that way. Even if you don't believe in Judaism, you, my friend, are still a Jew. You can't really opt out of it.

Maybe that's why Jews are Jew*ish*. It's more vague and casts a wider net than other religions. "I'm a Hindu." "I'm a Muslim." "I'm Jew . . . ish." Less commitment is involved when "ish" is in the mix. I'm not starving. I'm hungry-ish. I'm not freezing. I'm cold-ish. I'm not a Jew, but I'm for sure

Jew*ish*. Who isn't? Even Idris Elba does some things that are Jew*ish*.

And, to my first point, I can't deny the Jew breeding theory works. My sister met her husband at Jew camp, and my two Jewish nephews are the direct result of this Jew expansion strategy, which will hopefully lead to what we Jews refer to as Jewtopia.

My particular Jewish summer camp, Camp Miriam, was modeled after a kibbutz, which is kinda like a Jewish commune. On a kibbutz, everyone has a job, and in exchange you get room and board, education for your kids, and some extra cash. So, in summer-camp form, you get a place where the entire infrastructure—from the cooking to the cleaning to the maintenance—is handled by kids aged eight to fifteen and led by counselors aged seventeen to nineteen, which, looking back, is batshit fucking insane. It's like leaving your dog in the care of a slightly bigger dog in a facility that is managed by other dogs of various sizes. That analogy ran out of steam fast, but you get the idea.

My first year going, when I was ten, I got a job in the kitchen as a dishwasher, operating one of those industrial contraptions that is about the size of a pinball machine with a giant guillotine door that you raise and lower with a big handle. It made me feel very adult, mostly because I was doing a job that absolutely should only have been done by an adult.

I did not clean those dishes well. The fact that the entire camp didn't die of some sort of dysentery is amazing and really bucks some stereotypes about Jewish immune systems.

For the most part, the counselors were the sons and daughters of Vancouver hippies, but every once in a while we got an Israeli fresh out of the army who seemed bent on repaying whatever *Full Metal Jacket*–type hazing they'd received on soft Canadian Jewish boys, the absolute softest of all Jewish boys, who are already predisposed to being soft as fuck. Israeli Jews are different. They're not fluffy like North American Jews. They're sinewy and leathery. They have bodies like Madonna: veiny, lean, and immersed in the ways of Kabbalah. Also, they're aggressive, and they would essentially torture us, using three demented techniques that I assume were cooked up by Mossad agents hoping to extract sensitive information.

The first is the Typewriter, which involves pinning your child victim to the ground with a knee over each of his arms to incapacitate him. You then tap on the child's chest, HARD, as though you are Tom Hanks testing out a vintage Imperial, and then SLAP the child in the face to reset the reel. (Yes, that is a reference to Tom Hanks's well-known love of antique typewriters.)

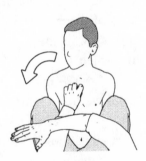

The next is the Waffle, which requires a racket of some sort—tennis, badminton, whathaveyou—and a hairbrush. Subdue the child in a similar manner to the Typewriter; lay the racket across his bare chest, or back, or anywhere, really; then scrub over the area with the brush. Remove the racket, and you have a waffle.

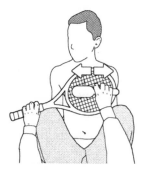

The last is the Windmill, which requires a broom handle, baton, yardstick, or something of the sort. Wedgie the small defenseless Jewish child to the degree that their underpant leg holes are exposed ABOVE the waistband of their Umbro shorts.

Then weave the broom handle (or other implement) *through* the exposed leg holes.

And now TWIST.

Once the traumatized Jewish child's screams reach a deafening point, release. If all has gone right, the elasticity of the child's underpants should unwind, causing the broom handle to spin like a windmill.

I learned every swear word there is at camp (I thought "cock" was a vagina up until then, so that was valuable information), made friends I still have to this day, and can still operate most industrial dishwashing equipment fairly competently. Remarkably, this place that basically amounted to a Jewish *Lord of the Flies* (*Lord of the Ryes? Lord of the Matzoh Breis?* I'll workshop this.) went largely without incident.

That is, if you overlook the terrible, terrible incident that happened in 1997.

Halfway through every summer, we would go on what was known as Tiyul, which was essentially a three-night camping trip. Now, as much as Jews love *camp,* I'd say they generally have an inverse relationship with camp*ing,* which is a VERY different activity. Camp had a swimming pool, bathrooms, a tetherball court. *Camping* doesn't have jack-fucking-shit, and every year things would go wrong.

In '95 we were supposed to hike for five hours to a lake where we would camp, drinking water from the lake itself.

We hiked all day to get to the lake and, when we arrived, were alerted the lake had beaver fever, which not only rhymes but also involves the word "beaver" *and* makes you shit yourself for days on end, so it's hands down the most hilarious of diseases; but at the time, it wasn't cool. We couldn't camp there, so we hiked BACK to our starting point, which was the parking lot of a ski resort, where we slept until a bus could be organized to come pick us up. "Can't get much worse than this!"

In '97, we were fifteen and our counselors were seventeen, which, again, is like entrusting a kitten to a ferret. The plan for Tiyul was needlessly ambitious. We were to take a ferry to Vancouver Island and hike the Juan de Fuca Trail, which is a TWENTY-NINE-MILE trail that winds along the forested mountainous coast. There are no services anywhere along the trail, and its current website describes it as "difficult and strenuous for a four-day hike." We were gonna do it in three, which meant we needed to do about ten hours of hiking a day.

The first day was hard but not yet disastrous. It drizzled as we camped out under tarps on Mystic Beach, and in the middle of the night, we snuck out into the woods to eat a giant bag of Sour Patch Kids, which were contraband.

The next morning, we started early. British Columbia is technically a rainforest, which might sound odd—until you're trudging through one of its many forests as it pisses rain. The already "difficult and strenuous" hike was becoming "super fucking hard and pretty fucking dangerous." The trail turned into slippery mud.

Because it's the worst possible thing that could have happened, we were halfway through the second day of our three-day hike, putting us fourteen miles into the twenty-nine-mile trail, making our way across a narrow cliffside in a single-file line, when I heard one of the counselors, Jono, yell, "EVERY-BODY STOP AT THE CLEARING UP AHEAD!"

We gathered in a little seaside ravine and another counselor, Zoey, came running up to the group of us, roughly twenty-five kids. She looked spooked.

"Aviva Strubisky fell. She sprained her ankle really fucking bad and passed out from the pain."

I went to elementary school with Aviva, and this added up. Once, paramedics had to come to give her smelling salts in Hebrew class in fourth grade because she fainted. Also, I had a crush on Aviva, so I was particularly invested in her and her consciousness and her ankle and her overall well-being. We bombarded Zoey with questions.

MAYAN BOMSHTICK: Is it bad?

ZOEY: We don't know. She's unconscious.

SAUL MOSCOVITCH: That seems pretty fucking bad!

LAUREN HERSHFIELD: What do we do?

ZOEY: I don't fucking know!

MAYAN BOMSHTICK: Well, if you don't fucking know, then who DOES fucking know?

ZOEY: I don't fucking know!

SAUL MOSCOVITCH: Well, what the fuck?

ZOEY: Yeah! What the fuck is right!

Jono yelled from up the trail, "She's awake!!"

Zoey ran off, leaving us with another counselor, Dan, a very sensitive lefty Jew. He was starting to hyperventilate a little. All the campers looked at each other, and I'm pretty sure all of us were thinking: *Remember when Dan broke down crying as he sang Indigo Girls at the campfire last Friday? Yeah, he's not gonna deal with this well.*

Zoey ran back. "She's awake, but she can't walk."

Saul Moscovitch started to freak out a bit. "Great! We're gonna fucking DIE out here!!"

Yiron, an Israeli kid who barely spoke English, went up to Zoey. "I am good in woods and forest. I will go to find service road. I will get help."

Dan, the sensitive lefty, seemed to be nearing a panic attack and jumped at the chance to be active. "YES. Perfect. You all wait here. And me and Yiron will come back with help."

Before anyone could settle on whether it was actually a good idea or not, they marched out into the woods, and I was 99 percent sure I'd never see them again.

Zoey unzipped her backpack and produced a signal flare, the kind where you pull a string and it shoots an orange ball of fire in the air. "If we see a boat on the coast, we can shoot this off. We only have one, though."

I thought, *Wow, this is a real emergency if we're resorting to signal flares.* And I also thought, *Please, god, let me shoot off the signal flare.* I'd only seen them in movies, and although it was a clear sign of how dire things were, I thought it was cool as fuck.

"Don't worry," Zoey said. "Yiron and Dan will be back with help soon!"

Five hours later and Yiron and Dan still hadn't come back. I pictured Yiron eating Dan's corpse in the woods but then realized Dan's corpse wouldn't technically be kosher, so he probably wouldn't do that. The mood was shifting from "this is a crazy story" to "wow, this is a potentially fucked-up story." The rain was pouring down harder than ever, and a few of the kids were beginning to show signs of hypothermia. Zoey pulled me and Ben, my best friend, away from the group.

"Jono wants to talk to you two."

We followed her about five minutes back up the trail, and the whole time I'm thinking, *What do they want with me? Did they single me out as the leader of the kids? The smartest of the group, being invited into some sort of think tank to figure out how to handle things?*

We rounded a narrow rock corner and saw Jono with Aviva, who was lying in the mud, going in and out of consciousness. Jono produced a small ax and thrust it into my hand. He looked at me and Ben. "You're the two largest kids in the group. Chop down two trees. We're gonna lay a tarp over them and make a stretcher and carry her out the way we came."

ME: What do you mean?

JONO: You heard me.

BEN: I've never chopped down a fucking tree.

JONO: Nobody here has, obviously!

(Jews.)

ME: We can't carry her out of here!

BEN: We couldn't even walk to here without someone getting hurt, and we weren't yet carrying an injured person, which I assume will make this whole shit a lot fucking harder.

JONO: There's no other plan. We gotta get out of here.

It took us about thirty minutes to chop down the first tree, which was around the thickness of my arm. We hacked it into an eight-foot piece, which we could barely lift on our own.

I looked at Ben. "Yo, dude, this is only one half of the stretcher and there's no teenage girl lying in it yet. How the fuck are we gonna carry the whole thing out? We can barely carry this."

"Maybe once she's in there, the weight will distribute it all out properly."

I didn't really know what the fuck that meant, but at the time, it seemed to make sense.

A half hour later, tree number two came down, and it was getting dark. The girls in the group had started to burn their tampons for warmth, as they were the only dry and flammable things we had. We tied the tarp to our tree trunks and laid our stretcher next to Aviva, who was shivering as her eyes rolled back in her head. Me, Jono, Ben, and Zoey heaved Aviva into the stretcher. We gripped the trunks and hoisted, lifting her off the wet ground. We all looked at each other. "Alright, we've got a rough twelve hours ahead of us, but we can DO this if we work together and don't give up."

We started the march, and after three steps, Jono slipped in the mud, sending Aviva to the ground with a THUD.

"Fuck, sorry! Sorry! Sorry! Aviva, you okay?"

(Pained grumble.)

"Great. Alright. Let's try again."

We all gripped the stretcher. "This is gonna be harder than we thought, but we got this. Let's DO it!!"

Again, we hoisted. Again, we walked a few steps, and again, we slipped, ate shit, and dropped Aviva in the cold mud from, like, three feet off the ground.

It had been twenty minutes and we'd moved about seven feet and arguably fucked Aviva up more than she'd already been fucked up, and she was already pretty fucked up. This shit just didn't seem like it was gonna happen.

And then I saw something. On the horizon, out on the ocean, lights! It was a ship! Miles and miles away, but there it was!

It was my moment.

"Give me the signal flare!!!"

Zoey reached into her bag and slammed it into my hand.

I leapt to the edge of the cliff, held the flare high above my head with one hand, gripped the rip cord with the other, and YANKED.

Now, if I had to list the most disappointing moments of my life—which I don't, but if I did—they would be:

1. Seeing the *Super Mario Bros.* movie in the theater as a child

2. Meeting George Lucas

3. This shit with the signal flare

What looked like a half-lit candle rose about twenty feet in the air and then crashed down into the ocean below. It was so unremarkable, there was no chance that the ship saw it. I barely saw it and it happened right in front of me.

We were fucked. I remember thinking, *If we die out here, maybe they'll rename the trail after us? That would be nice.* (Juan de Jew-Ca Trail? I'll workshop this, too.)

Then we heard footsteps from up the trail. They got louder and louder until FOUR GIANT, BEAUTIFUL, STRONG men in their fifties came around the corner. In my head today, they all looked like Captain "Sully" Sullenberger, the dude who heroically landed a plane in the Hudson River and is the subject of an insane Clint Eastwood film where the climax happens five minutes into the movie.

The four men stopped in their tracks.

SULLY 1: What's happened?
SULLY 2: Is there a problem?

Jono approached the Sullies (Sullii?). "Yeah. This girl hurt her ankle and went into shock. Can you help?"

Sully 3 stepped forward. "Of course we can. We're god-damn fucking firemen!"

I'm SURE that he didn't actually say it like that, but it felt like he did. And they were, for real, goddamn fucking fire-men.

The Sullii instantly sprang into action, as a Fireman Sully is wont to do. "There's a service road one kilometer from here. We can carry her using this stretcher you guys made."

BOOYAH. I'm a hero.

SULLY 4: Just give us five minutes to rebuild it and make it functional.

Fuck you, Sullies. I thought we had a good thing going.

SULLY 1: It's great you guys stayed together. Very smart. The worst thing you could have done is split up.

JONO: Yeah . . . uh . . . well, technically, we did, I guess . . . split up . . . a bit.

SULLY 2: What in the name of god do you mean?

JONO: Another counselor and camper went off into the woods to try to find help. You didn't see them as you were coming, did you?

SULLIES 1 AND 2: No!

JONO: Fuck.

SULLY 3: There are two kids out there?

JONO: Well, a kid and a counselor.

SULLY 3: How old is the counselor?

JONO: . . . Seventeen?

SULLY 3: Oh no! That's two kids!

It dawned on us that Yiron and Dan being lost in the woods might actually be way, way worse of a situation than Aviva being passed out on the path. The Sullenbergers led us about forty minutes through the woods, carrying Aviva in a way that was so effortless, it made me legitimately mad. The whole time, they were questioning the possible whereabouts of the missing kids.

SULLY 4: Did they say which way they were going?

JONO: Uh . . . no.

SULLY 1: Did they have a map or anything?

JONO: Uh . . . no.

The Sullenbergerses (sp?) led us up and over a small rocky face, where we found a dark, abandoned trucker's road.

SULLY 2: Alright, now we trek up the road and maybe we can flag down a—

The flashing of emergency lights became visible in the distance. Around the bend came an ambulance, and, even better, Yiron and Dan were in the front seat! Not only did they not die, they came with help!

Sort of.

Dan and Yiron had somehow made it to the main road, hitchhiked to a nearby small-town hospital, and got their *one* ambulance and a single emergency pickup truck to come and help us. Aviva was loaded in, along with Abby Saltzberg and Lauren Hershfield, who were showing signs of hypothermia.

"Alright, we're gonna take them back to the hospital."

"What about us?!"

The ambulance driver looked over at the remaining freezing, wet children. He clearly had no clue what to do. I guess the magnitude of the situation was kinda hard to comprehend. A lot had to go wrong to make thirty people need rescuing, and a lot did. We needed a bus or something, and I guess that wasn't easy on short notice.

The ambulance driver turned to the dude in the pickup truck: "Chris, you stay with them. Help them till we're able to get enough resources together to get everyone to safety."

Chris was maybe twenty and looked like a young James Marsden, which was to say, he was *not* Jewish, which at this point, was very comforting. The last Gentiles we'd encountered had been immensely helpful.

Chris looked at us, and again, somehow, me and Ben were chosen, because, again, I think at that age, height becomes associated with skill and intelligence. I've always been pretty tall, which I took for granted until I recently tried to set up my short friend.

"How tall is he?" my female friends would ask, often before any other questions.

"What does that matter?" I was offended on his behalf. "He's short! Who cares?"

"Easy for you to say. I gotta date a short dude and always wonder—was there a taller version of this same dude out there somewhere?"

Brutal, but good point.

On this particular day, my height made me seem capable and maybe slightly more mature than the other kids, which Chris would soon see was very far from the case.

He addressed the group. "Alright, I'm gonna take these two guys in my truck to the lot up the road, which is a five-minute walk. We're gonna start a fire, and by the time you all get there, we'll have it set up to keep you warm until they can get a bus to take you all somewhere safe."

Me and Ben climbed into the front of the pickup truck. We rounded the bend and pulled into a big dirt lot.

CHRIS: **Make a pile of wood!**

BEN: **It's all wet, dude!**

CHRIS (WITH CHRISTIAN SWAGGER): **Don't worry!**

We threw all the branches and logs we could find in a big pile while Chris went to the truck. He came back with a bright-red canister about the size of a bowling pin. It said GASOLINE in black letters on the side.

"Alright, get back."

Chris doused the pile with gas and tossed in a match. It roared to life, but because it was still raining like crazy, it instantly started to die out. So Chris dumped more gas on the fire, but this time, the fire crawled up the stream of pouring gas, reaching the can, engulfing it in flames.

CHRIS (SHOCKED): **Fuck!**

He dropped the flaming can, which started rolling back toward the pickup truck, where it would very clearly settle to a stop directly underneath the gas tank, blowing up the truck and likely killing us all.

CHRIS: **Stop it!**

ME: **How?!**

CHRIS: **Grab it!**

ME: **It's on fire!**

It kept rolling toward the truck. I had to act.

I ran up and KICKED the gas can as hard as I could away from the truck, sending it bouncing across the parking lot, leaving a thirty-foot-long, eight-foot-tall wall of flames behind it. The rest of the campers came around the bend and were shocked to see what I imagine looked like a solid episode of *Game of Thrones,* though they were over a decade away from understanding that awesome reference.

Although unruly, the fire wall kept us warm until a series of fire trucks showed up and took us to a fire station, where they had cots and soup and those thick wool blankets you see in disaster movies. We weren't at "shiny foil blanket" level disaster, which I'm still thankful for, because once those shiny foil blankets come out, you know the shit has really hit the fan.

They eventually took us to a hotel, where we got to use a pay phone to call our parents and spend the night before we were all taken back to camp. We were on the local news and our rescue was officially deemed a "provincial emergency."

Dan, the lefty Jew, had a meltdown when we got back and left for three days to get his mind together. Aviva was back at camp after two days, and she seemed impressed that I helped build a stretcher. Thankfully, her memory of being dropped several times was foggy.

It's an event that I always had a hard time contextualizing. Were we really in danger? Was it just a taste of adventure in what was ultimately more of an inconvenient situation than a full-on disaster? There were maybe only one or two moments I was actually frightened over the course of the twelve-hour ordeal, and the moment that was by far the most terrifying was when I almost got exploded, which happened *after* we were rescued and was mostly my fault.

Recently, I reconnected with Jono, who's still a good friend of my sister. We hadn't talked in years, and pretty quickly after we saw each other, we started reminiscing about the camping trip. I told him how even though it was scary, I didn't feel like we were ever in any real danger, because he and the other counselors didn't seem that stressed out. Nobody did.

JONO: Really? That's not true at all. I was stressed as fuck. It completely traumatized me. It was one of the worst things that ever happened to me. I was 100 percent sure we were all gonna die out there.

ME: Yeah, but, when you think about it, it's still kind of a funny story, isn't it?

JONO: Nope . . . not at all.

ACKNOWLEDGMENTS

'd like to thank Mark, Sandy, Danya, Max, Joe, Gideon, Lauren, and Zelda for being my wonderful and loving family without whom I could not function.

SETH ROGEN is a comedian, actor, writer, producer, and director. He's known for his roles in *The Lion King, Long Shot,* and *Knocked Up.* With his writing partner, Evan Goldberg, he co-wrote *Superbad* and *Pineapple Express,* and directed *This Is the End* and *The Interview,* all of which Rogen starred in. He lives in California with his wife, Lauren Miller, and their dog, Zelda.

yearbookthebook.com

ABOUT THE TYPE

This book was set in Scala, a typeface designed by Martin Majoor in 1991. It was originally designed for a music company in the Netherlands and then was published by the international type house FSI FontShop. Its distinctive extended serifs add to the articulation of the letterforms to make it a very readable typeface.